REWARD

Upper-intermediate

Grammar and Vocabulary Workbook

Simon Greenall
Diana Pye

MACMILLAN
HEINEMANN
English Language Teaching

Macmillan Heinemann English Language Teaching, Oxford

A division of Macmillan Publishers Limited

Companies and representatives throughout the world

ISBN 0 435 24272 5 (with key)

ISBN 0 333 74273 7 (without key)

Text © Simon Greenall 1998

Design and illustration © Macmillan Publishers Limited 1998

Heinemann is a registered trademark of Reed Educational and Professional Publishing Limited

First published 1998

Author's Acknowledgements
The author would like to thank Diana Pye for her invaluable contribution to this material.

Designed by Sarah Nicholson

Printed and bound in Great Briatin by Scotprint Ltd, Musselburgh

98 99 00 01 02 10 9 8 7 6 5 4 3 2 1

Contents

Lessons 1–3

VOCABULARY

1 Match a word on the left with a word on the right that has a similar meaning.

1	rules	a	supporter
2	manner	b	admit
3	current	c	rival
4	fan	d	intimate
5	holy	e	hobby
6	close	f	grin
7	deliberately	g	field
8	opponent	h	code
9	confess	i	sacred
10	smile	j	on purpose
11	pastime	k	way
12	pitch	l	present

2 Complete the sentences with words from the left-hand column of activity 1. You may have to change some of the words slightly.

1 The player was sent off because he _____ kicked the goalkeeper.
2 They are both fanatical football _____. They never miss a match.
3 She was severely reprimanded for breaking the _____.
4 He has such a charming _____ that even his _____ like him.
5 He _____ to having broken the law on three occasions.
6 They have had a very long and _____ relationship.
7 The _____ champions are Barcelona and Madrid.
8 When the two teams ran on to the _____ the crowd shouted and waved flags.

3 Circle the odd-one-out.

1 cuddle   pinch   smile   laugh   grin
2 rule   norm   opportunity   code   convention
3 kiss   hug   handshake   bow   kick
4 pilgrim   pitch   faithful   icon   cathedral
5 team   goal   chew   score   league
6 event   mistake   learn   correct
7 knees   thumb   foreigner   back   neck
8 think   know   perform   understand   learn

4 Match the definitions with the odd-ones-out in activity 3.

a a place where you can play football. _____
b an organised occasion. _____
c to break something up with your teeth. _____
d someone who comes from a different country from you. _____
e to squeeze someone with your finger and thumb. _____
f to hit someone or something with your foot. _____
g a situation in which you can do something you might find interesting or useful. _____
h to do an action or a task. _____

5 The verbs below describe actions. Write down the parts of the body you use to perform the actions.

blow	*mouth, nose*	pat	_____
bow	_____	point	_____
chew	_____	scratch	_____
clap	_____	shrug	_____
frown	_____	stare	_____
grin	_____	wave	_____
kiss	_____	wink	_____
nod	_____	yawn	_____

6 Match the two parts of the sentences.

1 He didn't answer my question, [d]
2 In Japan you bow [ ]
3 You clap [ ]
4 He frowned [ ]
5 He acknowledged them [ ]
6 In most countries it is rude [ ]
7 They waved [ ]
8 You yawn when [ ]
9 She kissed [ ]
10 He patted [ ]

a at the end of a performance to show your appreciation.
b goodbye to us.
c her son goodnight.
d he just shrugged his shoulders.
e when you greet someone.
f you are tired or bored.
g the dog.
h to point your finger at someone.
i with a nod.
j with displeasure.

7 Put the words under the correct heading. Some words may go under more than one heading.

address attend awe-inspiring cheek
coincidence commentary customs deadly
electric fail frantic forgivable gesture
heart kneel laugh native profitable strict
suspicious vary

Verb	Adjective	Noun
address	_____	*address*
_____	_____	_____
_____	_____	_____
_____	_____	_____
_____	_____	_____
_____	_____	_____
_____	_____	_____

8 Use the word in brackets to form a word that fits in the space.

1 In some countries it is quite _____ for men to greet each other by exchanging kisses. (accept)
2 However, in many countries it is considered _____ for a man to kiss a woman in public. (insult)
3 They have known each other since _____. (child)
4 Their _____ has survived over the years and now at the age of seventy they are still very close. (friend)
5 In the 19th century children were expected to be seen and not heard. Bad _____ was severely punished. (behaviour)
6 The language course I went on last summer was linguistically and culturally very _____. (reward)
7 He writes very good English but he really needs to improve his _____ mastery of the language because he will be travelling a lot more for his company in the future. (speak)
8 I made a number of interesting _____ when I was staying in London. (acquaint)
9 I _____ her immediately even though I hadn't seen her for over ten years. (recognise)
10 Football is one of Italy's most _____ industries. (profit)

9 Complete the sentences.

1 We are really looking *f*_____ to starting our English course.
2 You are *e*_____ to conform to the social code.
3 Most people are not *w*_____ by foreigners' mistakes.

4 If you ever get the *o*_____, I advise you to go and see a big football match. You won't regret it.

5 How do you *a*_____ your friends and acquaintances?

6 Social *c*_____ in Germany are quite strict.

7 Can you *g*_____ what a word means from the context?

8 I'm afraid I've *f*_____ how to say that in English. Can you help me?

10 Complete the sentences with a question word.

when	where	why	how
what	which	who	

1 She doesn't know _____ to get there.

2 It's so foggy they can't see _____ is in front of them.

3 She can't decide _____ to go for her holiday this summer.

4 They both look alike. I can't tell _____ is mine.

5 I don't know _____ they are. I've never even seen them before.

6 I'm not sure _____ it starts. You'd better phone the cinema.

7 It's 10 o'clock! _____ are you so late?

11 Put the words in the right order and make questions.

1 to/know/it/polite/stare/at/someone/you/don't/is/?

_____

2 you/should/you/hands/goodbye/when/say/shake/?

_____

3 mistake/you/have/made/a/social/ever/?

_____

4 do/greet/you/friends/how/close/?

_____

5 in/public/blow/it/your/to/is/rude/nose/?

_____

6 you/big/football/like/to/a/would/see/match/?

_____

7 women/is/with/popular/both/men/football/and/?

_____

8 last/won/Cup/who/the/World/?

_____

12 Answer the questions in activity 11.

1 _____

2 _____

3 _____

4 _____

5 _____

6 _____

7 _____

8 _____

GRAMMAR

1 Cross out the mistakes and write the correct questions underneath.

1 Did you ever been to an English-speaking country?

_____

_____

2 Where can you hear speaking English in your country?

_____

_____

3 Does he ever uses his native language during the English class?

_____

_____

4 Who does speak to you most during the lesson? Your teacher or your fellow students?

_____

_____

5 Are you looking to forward to this English course?

_____

_____

6 You didn't start learning English at primary school, didn't you?

_____

_____

7 Can you to understand native speakers?

_____

8 Have you ever attend a football match?

_____

9 Should you to shake hands with people each time you meet them in your country?

_____

_____

10 Is there any sports which attract huge crowds in your country?

_____

_____

2 Answer the questions in activity 1.

1 _____

2 _____

3 _____

4 _____

5 _____

6 _____

7 _____

8 _____

9 _____

10 _____

3 Write suitable questions for these answers. Use the words in brackets.

1 (far)_____

It's about four miles from the centre of town.

2 (cinema)_____

Yes, that's a good idea. What film shall we see?

3 (new teacher)_____

He seems very nice indeed.

4 (do)_____

No, I try to avoid using my own language during English lessons.

5 (English-speaking country)_____

_____

Yes, I've been to the United States twice on exchange visits.

6 (much)_____

I spend most of my spare time cycling.

7 (social norms)_____

Yes, definitely. I think it's very important to try and conform to the unwritten rules.

8 (find)_____

Yes, I'm sure it's easier for children to learn a foreign language.

9 (long)_____

It takes about two hours.

10 (shopping)_____

No, I'm afraid I didn't have time yesterday. I'll do it tomorrow morning.

4 Complete the passage with the indefinite or definite article.

There were four people including myself in (1)____ compartment. Sitting by (2)____ window was (3)____ lady in her sixties. When I entered (4)____ compartment she looked up from (5)____ newspaper she was reading and smiled at me. She had (6)____ interesting face which attracted me immediately. There was (7)____ young boy of about fifteen years old who was accompanied by (8)____ elderly man. They were having (9)____ heated discussion about something in (10)____ sporting magazine.

Suddenly (11)____ compartment door burst open and (12)____ tall fair-haired man came in. He was out of breath because, as he explained to me later, he had almost missed (13)____ train and had been obliged to run from (14)____ taxi rank to (15)____ platform. (16)____ train was just moving off when he jumped on it. I recognised (17)____ man immediately. I had just attended (18)____ two-day conference and we had been staying at (19)____ same hotel. I couldn't recall his name but I remembered that he was (20)____ chemical engineer from Southampton. He acknowledged my smile with (21)____ broad grin. 'That's (22)____ bit of luck! You don't

mind if I sit with you, do you? I wasn't looking forward to (23)____ eight hour journey on my own. Perhaps we could have (24)____ chat to while away the time. Did you enjoy (25)____ conference? I wasn't very impressed with (26)____ new organisation ...'

5 Complete the sentences with a suitable question word or tag.

1 Let's take the afternoon off, _____?
2 _____ you come? You'd really enjoy it.
3 You aren't following the evening course, _____?
4 It's easy to forget a language if you don't practise it, _____?
5 Give this to your teacher, _____?
6 You didn't miss the train, _____?
7 He makes so many social mistakes, _____?
8 You haven't seen Don this afternoon, _____?
9 There'll be plenty of opportunities to meet people, _____?
10 Listen to this, _____?

WRITING

1 Complete these sentences and make statements about learning English and your English class.

1 The best way to learn a language is ...

_____

2 What I find particularly difficult is ...

_____

3 The best way to ...

_____

4 It's important to ...

_____

5 You are expected to …

_____

6 You aren't supposed to …

_____

7 Don't worry about …

_____

8 You should use a _____ if _____

_____

9 I need a lot of practice in …

_____

10 I particularly enjoy …

_____

11 I hope I'll …

_____

12 I'd like to …

_____

2 Choose a sport and a pastime you particularly enjoy. Write down words and expressions you could use to talk about these activities.

_____

_____

_____

_____

_____

3 Answer the questions about one of the activities you like.

1 How did you become interested in this activity? _____

_____

2 Where do you practise it?

_____

_____

3 Is it a passion or just a pleasurable pastime?

_____

_____

4 Have you had any formal lessons or been on a course?

_____

_____

5 Have you met other people who have the same interest?

_____

_____

6 How competent are you?

_____

_____

7 Do you hope to achieve anything in particular or is it just for pleasure?

_____

_____

8 Do you take part in competitions?

_____

_____

4 Write a letter to a friend telling him or her about your particular interest. Think about the questions in activity 3. Encourage your friend to take up the sport or pastime.

Lessons 3-5

VOCABULARY

1 Put the words under the correct headings. Some words may go in more than one group.

acting race applaud marathon landmark
guide audience stage winner play
running museum lose scene jumping
performance visit stadium company track
final palace building

Theatre	Athletics	Sightseeing
_____	_____	_____
_____	_____	_____
_____	_____	_____
_____	_____	_____
_____	_____	_____
_____	_____	_____
_____	_____	_____
_____	_____	_____
_____	_____	_____
_____	_____	_____

2 Write down words you could use to talk about the following topics under the headings.

Football	Shopping	Travelling by train
_____	_____	_____
_____	_____	_____
_____	_____	_____
_____	_____	_____
_____	_____	_____

3 Match the sentences 1-6 with the sport or leisure activity they refer to.

watching television dancing skiing fishing
politics football

1 All they do is kick a ball around. _____
2 He just sits on the river bank all day. _____
3 If only he didn't watch those awful
   soap operas! _____
4 I wish he'd spend more time at
   home and less at meetings. _____
5 All they do is queue up for ages in
   the snow. It only takes them a few
   minutes to get back down. _____
6 She's always going out to the disco. _____

4 Match a word on the left with a word on the right.

1 top	a measure
2 winding	b home
3 rainy	c food
4 higher	d minority
5 cost-saving	e meal
6 ethnic	f floor
7 spicy	g education
8 sharp	h dramatics
9 four-course	i store
10 amateur	j lane
11 stately	k frost
12 chain	l season

5 Use the word in brackets to form a word that fits in the space.

1 The _____ of the peace talks
   highlights the limitations of American
   diplomacy.   (fail)
2 The town itself isn't particularly interesting
   but the _____ are beautiful.
   (surround)
3 The _____ was so good that the
   audience gave them a standing ovation.
   (perform)
4 The lecture was so _____ that a
   number of students fell asleep.   (bore)

5 The dinner party was very _____. (succeed)

6 She won the best _____ of the year award. (act)

7 She is not a virtuoso but she is certainly a very _____ pianist. (accomplish)

8 The identity of the _____ guest of the show was kept a secret until the last minute. (celebrate)

9 The liberating army marched _____ into the capital. (triumph)

10 To my _____ most of the class passed the exam. (satisfy)

11 The _____ was deafening when she walked onto the stage. (applaud)

12 The music was so _____ that tears started running down her cheeks. (move)

6 Complete the sentences with the best word: a, b, c or d.

1 We could go for a _____ through the historic quarter before dinner this evening.
a wander b trip c stroll d cruise

2 The _____ of life in New York city is much faster than it is in the surrounding country.
a speed b pace c rush d hurry

3 They want to go sightseeing and they've asked me to organise an _____ for this afternoon.
a route b journey c way d itinerary

4 He wants a promotion so he's trying to _____ the boss by staying on at work after office hours.
a impress b determine c move d emphasise

5 It was really _____. I wouldn't have gone if I had known it was going to be so bad.
a lousy b hateful c bloated d pervasive

6 We have been living here for _____ too long now. It's time we moved.
a very b so c such d far

7 It was my first flight so I was _____ but not frightened at the prospect.

a impressed b apprehensive c confused d afraid

8 Grenoble which _____ in the Isère valley is surrounded by mountains.
a sits b site c lies d located

9 She goes to the gym three evenings a week to keep _____.
a up-to-date b fit c disciplined d healthy

10 She _____ the exam last week but she won't get the results until next month.
a passed b failed c took d achieved

7 Write a second sentence so that it has a similar meaning to the first sentence, using the words in brackets.

1 We have really had a very good time here this week. (enjoyed)

We_____

_____.

2 He just worries about his job all the time. (always)

He_____.

3 I gradually realised how much I loved the cottage in the hills. (fond)

I_____

_____

4 Our new neighbours are very noisy. (make)

Our_____.

5 I wish I had travelled more when I was young and fit. (regret)

I_____

_____.

6 When I see the sunset, I remember the past. (reminds)

Seeing_____.

7 He is heavily in debt to the bank.   (owes)

He_____.

8 He decided to resist temptation and revise for his exam.   (determined)

He_____

_____.

8 Complete these definitions with a suitable word.

1 An *o*_____ is someone who has a positive outlook on life.

2 A *p*_____ is someone who has a negative outlook on life.

3 A *g*_____ is a person who has obtained a university degree.

4 A person who is *s*_____ *c*_____ is someone who is very sure of himself or herself.

5 You reach a *c*_____ when you come to an agreement with someone but both parties give up something they originally wanted.

6 Someone who is *t*_____ at something is very good at it.

7 If someone is *d*_____ to do something they will not let anything stop them.

8 *F*_____ is a lack of success in doing something.

9 Would you expect to find these sentences and phrases in a formal or an informal letter? Write F for formal and I for informal.

1 Thanks for your letter.   _____
2 I would be grateful for your help in this matter.   _____
3 I look forward to hearing from you.   _____
4 See you soon.   _____
5 Yours faithfully,   _____
6 Dear Sir,   _____
7 Best wishes,   _____
8 Further to our conversation …   _____

9 I'm writing to say that I'll …   _____
10 I would very much appreciate it if you would …   _____

10 Use a suffix to write the adjectives which come from the following nouns and verbs.

coast	____	confuse	____	desert	____
determine	____	dust	____	fail	____
faith	____	haze	____	mountain	____
optimist	____	pound	____	profit	____
rain	____	rhythm	____	sand	____
scene	____	sleep	____	steam	____
success	____	talent	____	triumph	____
tropic	____	wealth	____		

11 Choose words from activity 10 and write five sentences.

_____

_____

_____

_____

_____

GRAMMAR

1 Some of the sentences are correct and some have a word which should not be there. Put a tick (✓) or write the word that should not be there in the space.

1 Will you ask to them to come after lunch?   _____
2 I have never seen anything like it.   _____
3 I chose that particular part of town on the purpose.   _____
4 They have never been gone to Brazil before.   _____
5 I just can't see the point of regretting the past.   _____

6 I couldn't to agree more.   _____

7 All they do is to argue all day long.   _____

8 I'll try and to get there this evening.   _____

2   Complete the dialogue with suitable words or phrases.

A   (1)_____ having a meal at the Fisherman's Lodge this evening? I (2)_____ pick you up at your flat and we (3)_____ go for a stroll along the river before dinner to work up an appetite.

B   I doubt if I (4)_____ be able to get out of work before seven. I've got a meeting with the marketing people.

A   Well, in that case, (5)_____ we meet down at the lodge and take it from there? I can always have a game of billiards while I'm waiting.

B   Yes, that would be better. I (6)_____ get there as early as I can.

A   (7)_____ I book a table?

B   Yes, I think you better had. They can be very busy on a Friday night.

A   What time (8)_____ I give them?

B   (9)_____ say half past eight, just to be on the safe side.

A   OK. I (10)_____ phone them this afternoon. See you this evening.

B   Bye.

3   Choose the best verb.

1 She has never *been taking/taken* a plane before.

2 We *have been standing/stood* here for an hour and they still haven't come.

3 He's *been knowing/known* her boyfriend for over a year now.

4 **A**   Why are you so wet?

   B   I *have been mending/have mended* the shower.

5 I *have only been reading/have only read* three of the books you lent me.

6 What *have you been doing/have you done?* There's paint all over the furniture.

7 *Have you been seeing/Have you seen* the new art museum on the left bank?

8 How long *have you been having/have you had* an au pair staying with you?

9 What *have you been doing/have you done* with the encyclopaedia? I can't find it anywhere.

10 We *haven't been visiting/haven't visited* the town yet. We *haven't been having/haven't had* time.

4   Match the functions 1–8 with the sentences a–o.

1 making suggestions

2 complaining

3 agreeing

4 enquiring

5 disagreeing

6 making a request

7 making an offer

8 refusing

a No, I can't accept that. You're oversimplifying the issue.   ☐

b No, I won't be able to do it. I'm sorry.   ☐

c Let's go away to the mountains this weekend, shall we?   ☐

d I can't do that. It's not right.   ☐

e Yes, I think you're right.   ☐

f Why don't we watch television for a change?   ☐

g Could you tell me what time the next bus leaves, please?   ☐

h I'll go out and get a take-away.   ☐

i Neither do I.   ☐

j   I'll take you to the station. ☐

k   He's always forgetting his books. ☐

l   No, that's rubbish. ☐

m   Will you ask them to come for nine o'clock instead of half past eight? ☐

n   She keeps asking me for money. ☐

o   Can you take a message, please? ☐

5   Complete the sentences in the correct tense using the verb in brackets.

1   I _____ (make) a number of trips to the States this year, but this is the last one.

2   I _____ (not, know) you were back! How long _____ (you, stay) in South America?

3   She _____ (grow) fond of the villagers and now she doesn't want to leave.

4   He _____ (read) that newspaper ever since he _____ (get) on the train in Santos.

5   We _____ (think) about your situation and we _____ (decide) to give you another chance.

6   Sorry I'm late. _____ (you, sit) here long?

7   She _____ (write) three novels in the last four years.

8   How many chocolates _____ (have) today?

6   Write sentences in the present perfect continuous or simple using the prompts.

1   How long/live/this town?

   _____

2   How many/new students/meet?

   _____

3   I/not know/director/very long.

   _____

4   They/study/chemistry/four years now.

   _____

5   How long/you/smoke?

   _____

6   How many/cigarettes/you smoke/today?

   _____

7   She/work/eight o'clock.

   _____

8   What/achieve/your life?

   _____

7   Complete the sentences with *will, won't* or *going to.*

1   We _____ stay at the Ritz, we've already booked a room.

2   I _____ call the police if you don't stop making a noise.

3   We _____ get there as soon as we are ready.

4   What _____ (you) do this weekend?

5   _____ (you) join us for a coffee?

6   We _____ visit the National Gallery this afternoon. _____ you join us?

7   I don't think I _____ have anymore, thank you.

8   What _____ (you) study next year?

8   Write sentences using *will.*

1   promise to drive carefully

   _____

2   refuse to do the washing up

   _____

3   ask someone to give you a lift into town

   _____

4   invite someone to stay for a cup of tea

   _____

5   offer to make the dinner

   _____

WRITING

1 Write five sentences with the pairs of words you formed in *Vocabulary* activity 3.

1 _____

2 _____

3 _____

4 _____

5 _____

2 Complete the statements for you.

1 I am particularly proud of _____

_____ .

2 I am usually apprehensive when _____

_____ .

3 I am not very optimistic about _____

_____ .

4 I am confident that _____

_____ .

5 I really admire _____ because _____

_____ .

6 I am very fond of _____

_____ .

7 I have never _____

_____ .

8 I feel very sad when _____

_____ .

9 I am determined _____

_____ .

10 I have always wanted _____

_____ .

3 Answer these questions about your home town or village.

How big is it?

_____

How old is it?

_____

What historical buildings or sites are there?

_____

Where is it situated?

_____

What is the climate like?

_____

What is the surrounding country like?

_____

What striking features are there?

_____

What is the general atmosphere?

_____

What nightlife is there?

_____

4 Write a letter to someone from another country who is coming to stay with you for the first time. Include a short description of your home town/village. Explain how to get there.

Lessons 6–8

VOCABULARY

1 Circle the odd-one-out.

1. surgeon doctor patient consultant nurse
2. dizzy shiver faint limp prescription
3. outpatients casualty surgery maternity hospital
4. bandage ointment hurt tablet plaster
5. cut wound pill injury sprain
6. cough heart attack sore throat accident flu
7. wheelchair pain crutches stick stretcher
8. blood heart anaesthetic throat stomach
9. death burial undertaker autopsy emergency
10. ears sight touch smell taste

2 Complete the sentences with the following words. There are five extra words.

outpatients casualty toothache disabled plaster sedative operations appointment pain injection prescription disease thermometer emergency ambulance

1. He's got a broken leg and he has to keep the _____ on for six weeks.
2. I went to the dentist's yesterday because I had a dreadful _____.
3. If you don't want to waste too much time it's a good idea to make an _____.
4. They gave her a _____ to calm her down.
5. The doctor made out a _____ for pain-killers.
6. He cut his finger so badly that I took him to _____ to have stitches.
7. He is so severely _____ that he has to have a wheelchair.
8. He caught some strange tropical _____ when he was abroad last summer.
9. I couldn't take my temperature because I couldn't find the _____.
10. Nowadays many _____ are performed under local anaesthetic.

3 Put the verbs under the correct heading according to whether they describe long or short actions.

gaze glance glimpse grab grasp hit hold kick listen nod notice nudge observe peer pinch punch snatch squeeze stare stroke watch

Long actions	Short actions
_____	_____
_____	_____
_____	_____
_____	_____
_____	_____
_____	_____
_____	_____
_____	_____
_____	_____
_____	_____
_____	_____

4 Complete the passage with words from activity 3. You may have to change the form of some of the words.

As I came out of the underground station, I (1) g_____ behind me. The man in black was standing by the ticket office (2) s_____ intently at someone or something near the opposite exit. He seemed to be watching a young man in a grey raincoat. The young man was (3) g_____ in my direction, but I don't think he could see me because of the crowd on the stairs. He put his hand inside his raincoat pocket and I caught a brief (4) *g*_____ of what looked like a gun. Suddenly, the man in black jumped over the central railing, (5) *g*_____ the young man's arm and (6) *s*_____the gun out of his hand. He then (7) *p*_____ him in the stomach several times, got up, ran to the exit and up into the street where he disappeared into the crowd. I turned my back on the scene in the tube station and walked on down the busy street.

5 Complete the sentences with the best word: a, b, c or d.

1 He was sleeping so _____ that I didn't like to disturb him.
   a soundly   b strongly   c hard   d softly

2 The door was slightly _____ but not enough for me to see who was in the room.
   a apart   b locked   c secured   d ajar

3 She _____ my hand comfortingly and told me not to worry.
   a pushed   b grasped   c squeezed
   d pinched

4 He _____ quickly at the headline then he put the newspaper down and turned towards me.
   a peered   b glanced   c gazed   d stared

5 She felt very uncomfortable because the woman at the counter was _____ rudely at her.
   a observing   b peeping   c staring
   d gazing

6 They spent the best part of an hour _____ up at the incredibly clear, night sky.
   a staring   b gazing   c glimpsing
   d glancing

7 There was the most unpleasant _____ imaginable coming from the main drains.
   a stink   b scent   c fragrance   d taste

8 The thief _____ her handbag and ran off down the street.
   a punched   b grasped   c gripped
   d snatched

9 She had fallen asleep in the middle of the lecture so I _____ her with my elbow.
   a nudged   b pinched   c winked
   d punched

10 I left the club early because the music was _____ and we couldn't hear ourselves talking.
   a noisy   b volume   c deafening
   d unpleasant

11 He _____ despondently through the rain looking thoroughly miserable.
   a shuffled   b trudged   c walked
   d strolled

12 The path was so wet and _____ that she could hardly keep on her feet.
   a greasy   b soft   c slippery   d sliding

6 Complete the sentences with a suitable adverb below. There are five extra adverbs.

cautiously   directly   gratefully   impulsively
intentionally   noisily   peacefully   rudely
scrupulously   skilfully   soundly   successfully
surprisingly   truthfully

1 He was sleeping _____.

2 They made sure the kitchen was _____ clean in case the health inspector came.

3 I accepted _____ his offer of help.

4 She was standing _____ opposite us so we could see her face clearly.

5 I advanced _____ through the dark room, trying not to make any a noise.

6 _____, I stopped the car and climbed up onto a rock which gave me a view of the coastline.

7 She completed her training course _____ and applied for a teaching job.

8 _____ , nobody seemed to think her behaviour was in any way suspicious.

9 I really didn't do it _____. It was an accident.

10 She had a reputation for operating quickly and _____ .

7 Write sentences with the five extra adverbs from activity 6.

1 _____

2 _____

3 _____

4 _____

5 _____

8 Use the word in brackets to form a word that fits in the space.

1 They _____ her of stealing but they had no proof.   (suspect)

2 She gave the patient a _____ to calm him down.   (sedate)

3 The _____ service took place on a bleak Saturday morning at the village cemetery. (bury)

4 Her _____was successful and only discovered when she died.   (deceive)

5 He took the waste-paper basket downstairs and _____ it into the dustbin.   (empty)

6 She _____ to run away from school on several occasions but her parents didn't take her _____ seriously.   (threat)

7 His results were so _____ that he decided to redo his final year.   (disappoint)

8 She felt _____ and unhappy when she first moved to the city.   (confuse)

9 The woman made a lasting _____ on everyone she met.   (impress)

10 There was such a _____ going on in the house opposite that they called the police. (disturb)

9 Match one of the following words with the definitions 1–15 below.

beach   cliff   crops   dry   estuary   farmland
fertile   fishing   footpath   harvest   hedge
hill   horizon   irrigation   jungle   lake
meadow   oasis   pass   peak   plain   range
river   rocks   rugged   slope   steep   stream
valley   vegetation   waterfall   wet   wood

1 A flat area between the sea and the land.   _____

2 A hot tropical forest with rich vegetation.   _____

3 A small river.   _____

4 Where a river meets the sea.   _____

5 A narrow track for walking through the countryside or the mountains.   _____

6 The top of a mountain.   _____

7 As far as the eye can see.   _____

8 When a river drops down a cliff it is called this.   _____

9 Land where crops are grown.   _____

10 A series of mountains.   _____

11 A 'natural' fence.   _____

12 The easiest way over a mountain.   _____

13 Where cattle graze.   _____

14 A welcome watering hole in the desert.   _____

15 A small scale forest.   _____

10 Write down words from activity 9 which you can use to talk about agriculture. Now think of five more words to add to the list.

_____   _____

_____   _____

_____   _____

_____   _____

_____

18

GRAMMAR

1 Rewrite these sentences with participle clauses.

1 I didn't want to upset her so I didn't mention the accident.

_____

_____

2 Because I woke up early, I went out for a walk.

_____

_____

3 As I crossed the park, I noticed my friend sitting on a bench.

_____

_____

4 Sherlock stood up suddenly and walked over to the window.

_____

_____

5 We followed the footpath which ran along the top of the cliff.

_____

_____

6 She spoke to the woman who was working in the garden.

_____

_____

7 Because I didn't want to go shopping, I ordered a pizza to be delivered.

_____

_____

8 She turned her head round slowly and caught a glimpse of the ghost.

_____

_____

2 Rewrite the following phrases using the nouns in *italics* as one element of a two-part adjective.

1 A boy who is six *years* old.

_____

2 A journey which takes two *hours*.

_____

3 A dinner with four *courses*.

_____

4 A film which lasts three *hours*.

_____

5 A golf course with eighteen *holes*.

_____

6 A hotel room which costs five hundred *pounds*.

_____

7 There are ten *storeys* in that office block.

_____

8 There are four *bedrooms* in that house.

_____

3 Rewrite these sentences in one sentence.

1 There is a new visitor centre in Culloden. It is excellent.

_____

_____

2 Loch Ness is a beautiful loch. It is long and narrow.

_____

3 Glencoe is a windswept mountain pass. It is breathtakingly beautiful.

_____

_____

4 Portree is a seaside tourist centre. It is a popular place.

_____

_____

5 Ben Nevis is 4,406 feet high. It is an unattractive mountain. It lies to the east of Fort William.

_____

_____

6 There is a ruined castle is at the top of a cliff. It is two hundred years old. It is spectacular.

_____

_____

7 There are sandy beaches. They are sheltered. They are wonderful.

_____

_____

8 There is a row of terraced houses above the harbour. They are freshly painted. They are picturesque.

_____

_____

4 Complete the sentences with a suitable preposition.

1 The turning to Maidenhead is halfway _____ the road from London to Oxford.

2 Edinburgh is _____ the east of Glasgow.

3 The Niagara Falls are about halfway _____ Lakes Ontario and Erie.

4 _____ either side of the pass there are rugged peaks.

5 The river winds its way peacefully _____ meadows and and cornfields.

6 On a clear day we can see the island of Lundy _____ the distance.

7 The lake is surrounded _____ bleak moorland.

8 The information centre is _____ the western side of the lake.

9 The road runs _____ our house.

10 The village is surrounded _____ fields.

5 Choose the best tense.

1 After they *had been/went* to the shops, they *went/had been* back to the hotel to get changed.

2 They *were driving/drove* along the main road when a police car *stopped/had stopped* them for speeding.

3 She *had been living/was living* in the nursing home for ten years when she *died/was dying*.

4 We *had been walking/were walking* in the mountains since morning when we finally *reached/were reaching* the hostel.

5 When she *passed/had passed* her Proficiency exam, she *had only been studying/was only studying* English for three years.

6 She *hasn't left/hasn't been leaving* the house since she *arrived/has arrived* home yesterday.

7 When they *got/had got* home, they realised that they *had forgotten/forgot* to buy eggs.

8 The man was exhausted when he fell because he *had been working/worked* too hard that week.

9 The patient was angry because he *had been waiting/was waiting* for over an hour.

10 He *had been running/had run* the business for forty years when he finally *retired/had retired* in the autumn.

11 He *has been running/had been running* the business for forty years now.

12 After Dr Green *had examined/had been examining* the patient, he told the nurse to administer a sedative.

6 **Rewrite these sentences with *Before* or *After* + -ing**

1 I applied for a job when I left college.

_____

2 I remembered to order dinner before I went out.

_____

3 When I had posted the letter, I went for a cup of coffee.

_____

4 When I had visited my mother in the ward, I talked to the consultant.

_____

_____

5 He studied for three years in York then he moved to London.

_____

_____

6 He worked as a waiter for a year then he went to live abroad.

_____

_____

7 He had a heart attack so he stopped smoking.

_____

8 When we had finished work, we went to the football match.

_____

_____

7 **Complete the passage with the verbs in brackets in the present perfect, past simple, past continuous, past perfect or the past perfect continuous.**

The only dinner party I (1)_____ (ever hold) was a complete disaster. I (2)_____ (never be) an accomplished cook so I thought it would be sensible to do something simple. I (3)_____ (see) a cooking programme on television the previous week and the chef (4)_____ (make) a seafood starter followed by, what appeared to be, a fairly straightforward casserole. The whole three-course meal only (5)_____ (take) him half an hour to prepare. Just what I needed! So I (6)_____ (go) to the fishmarket in the morning and (7)_____ (buy) some shrimps and mussels. I must say, they (8)_____ (not, look) fresh but the man said they (9)_____ (arrive) that morning and were straight out of the sea. I was desperate so I (10)_____ (buy) them. I (11)_____ (work) all afternoon on the meal. Running to the shop more than once to get missing ingredients, I (12)_____ (still, cook) when my guests (13)_____ (arrive). I hastily (14)_____ (put) the casserole in the oven to keep warm while we (15)_____ (have) a drink. We (16)_____ (chat) for over an hour when I suddenly (17)_____ (remember) that the casserole was still in the oven. Unfortunately, in my haste I (18)_____ (leave) it on high and the casserole (19)_____ (cook) away merrily for all that time. Needless to say it was ruined. Luckily there was the seafood starter and some very nice cheese.
The following day I (20)_____ (feel) very miserable when someone (21)_____ (phone) from the hospital. My three guests (22)_____ (take) there early that morning with food poisoning. I suppose I was lucky that I (23)_____ (not, have) time to eat any of the seafood! I (24)_____ (not, hold) another dinner party since then.

WRITING

1 Complete these sentences with information about yourself and people you know.

1 I don't like other people interfering in _____ .

2 I felt really good about _____ .

3 I like the way _____ .

4 It sounds silly but _____ .

5 I was impressed with _____ .

6 I'd like to spend time _____ .

7 _____ is in charge of _____ .

8 _____ is run by _____ .

9 I shall apply for _____ .

10 _____ would do me good.

2 Complete the sentences for you and your country.

1 If I had a sore throat I _____

_____ .

2 The last time I visited someone in hospital

_____

3 In my country, when there is an accident

_____

4 The last time I was ill, I _____

_____

5 To become a doctor you have to _____

_____ .

6 The health system is _____

_____

7 To see a doctor, you have to _____

_____

8 The last time I saw a doctor was _____

_____ .

3 Write a paragraph describing either an illness or an accident you had. Think about these questions.

- How did you feel?
- Was it serious?
- What treatment did you receive?
- What was the medical team like?
- How long did it take you to recover?
- Did you go to hospital?
- If so, what were your impressions?
- If not, how were you treated?

4 Write a short description of the countryside near where you live. If you live in the country, write about where your home is and the surrounding countryside. If not, choose a small town or a village you know and describe its setting. You can use words from *Vocabulary* activities 9 and 10.

Lessons 8–10

VOCABULARY

1 Match a word on the left with a word on the right with a similar meaning.

1	vacant	a	recall
2	protracted	b	condemn
3	reluctant	c	unpleasant
4	remember	d	empty
5	compulsory	e	inappropriate
6	dim	f	lengthy
7	illegal	g	catch
8	offensive	h	obligatory
9	unsuitable	i	agitation
10	capture	j	hesitant
11	convict	k	dark
12	tumult	l	prohibited

2 Use the word in brackets to form a word that fits in the space.

1 There is a _____ for a secretary at the travel agent's in High Street.   (vacant)

2 That hat isn't at all _____. It's much too formal.   (suit)

3 It is _____ to leave the grounds during school hours.   (forbid)

4 She was wearing a very _____ outfit.   (glamour)

5 Don't take your trainers off! You've got _____ feet!   (smell)

6 He made a _____ after a ten hour cross-examination.   (confess)

7 She didn't have her parents' _____ to stay out late on weekdays.   (permit)

8 After a moment's _____, the others followed him.   (hesitate)

9 The judge gave him a suspended sentence because it was his first _____.   (convict)

10 The headmaster said that her results were _____ but there was room for improvement.   (encourage)

3 Put the words under the correct headings.

aloud   bang   bright   caress   clang   colour   contact   creak   dark   deafening   dim   dingy   feel   gloomy   hard   hum   noisy   pat   ringing   rough   rustle   see   sticky   stroke   thud   tinkle   tumult

Light	Sound	Touch
_____	_____	_____
_____	_____	_____
_____	_____	_____
_____	_____	_____
_____	_____	_____
_____	_____	_____
_____	_____	_____

4 Complete the sentences with one of the following words. You may need to change the form of some of the words.

bark   creak   cry   gasp   groan   hiccup   rumble   rustle   sigh   slam   sniff   snore   thud   whistle

1 If you get _____, ask a friend to frighten you.

2 He was _____ so loudly that she nudged him with her elbow to wake him up.

3 The little girl was so upset that she _____ herself to sleep.

4 We tiptoed to our room but the floorboards _____ and woke our parents up.

5 They could hear a dog _____ somewhere down the road.

6 He _____ when the doctor said he had to stay in hospital for another week.

23

7 When I _____ , the dog came running towards me.

8 We could hear a distant _____ announcing yet another storm.

9 I could hear something _____ in the hedge so I stopped to see what it was.

10 She was _____ so I told her to blow her nose.

11 There was a _____ when something heavy fell onto the ground ahead of us.

12 She walked out of the room and _____ the door angrily.

13 She _____ in disbelief when she opened the box. There was a beautiful diamond necklace.

14 He _____ sadly and turned to leave. There was nothing he could do.

5   Match the two parts of the sentences.

1 I could hear
2 I could feel
3 I could see
4 I could smell

a them whispering to each other in the next room. ☐

b him coming down the path in his new suit. ☐

c something burning. ☐

d her hand gripping my arm in the dark. ☐

e someone humming in the bathroom. ☐

f the dinner cooking. ☐

g a child crying somewhere in the house. ☐

h the breeze on my face. ☐

i the bees buzzing. ☐

j them moving about in the distance. ☐

k the church bells ringing. ☐

6   Circle the odd-one-out.

1 illegal   unlawful   offence   crime   prohibited   truth

2 jury   judge   magistrate   witness   weapon   lawyer

3 innocent   prosecute   sentence   convict   charge   arrest

4 murder   blackmail   bail   mugging   burglary   arson

5 fine   trial   prison sentence   damages   caution   community service

6 thief   burglar   forger   barrister   drug dealer   shoplifter

7   Match these definitions with a word(s) from activity 6.

1 A person who saw a crime being committed.   _____

2 To deliberately set fire to a property.   _____

3 Someone who defends the accused in court.   _____

4 To sentence an offender to pay money.   _____

5 Against the law.   _____

6 Someone who steals from houses.   _____

7 A group of citizens who decide whether a defendant is guilty or not.   _____

8 To take legal action against someone.   _____

8   Complete the sentences.

1 He was *c*_____ of manslaughter and *s*_____ to two years in prison.

2 The *j*_____ found the man *g*_____ of pre-meditated murder.

3 In Britain, it is a criminal *o*_____ to carry a weapon.

4 There is always a *t*_____ by jury for serious crimes.

5 The policeman stopped the driver and *a*_____ him of dangerous driving.

6 The police dropped the *c*_____ against the woman because she had a good alibi.

7 The jury found the man *i*_____ and he was released.

8 It is against the *l*_____ to sell stolen goods.

9 Match the sentences with the replies.

1 Someone tried to break into my house in the night. I turned the lights on and they ran away. ☐

2 Why can't I fish in that river? ☐

3 Should I bring a cake or something? ☐

4 He was attacked by thieves and he fought back bravely. Unfortunately he is in hospital now. ☐

5 Do you need a licence to ride a bike in Britain? ☐

6 Are you allowed to drive a car before you are eighteen? ☐

a No, but you must have a licence to drive a car.

b He should have given them his money without resisting.

c No, you can't drive until you are eighteen.

d You don't need to bring anything.

e Nevertheless, you should have called the police. They may come again when you are out.

f Because you have to have a licence.

10 Choose one of the following adjectives to describe how you would feel in these situations.

outraged   amused   incredulous   frightened   unbelieving   sympathetic   astonished   hurt   overwhelmed   confident   inadequate   proud   depressed

1 If you saw a ghost. _____

2 If you came face to face with a burglar in your home at night. _____

3 Someone tells you about a ghost they have seen. _____

4 You witness a mugging. _____

5 A friend tells you about his or her personal problems. _____

6 You see someone writing graffiti on a freshly painted shop-front. _____

7 Someone you know says something false and offensive about you. _____

8 You are the only witness to a serious accident and your actions can save someone's life. _____

11 What would you do or not do in each of the situations in activity 10?

1_____

2_____

3_____

4_____

5_____

6_____

7_____

8_____

25

GRAMMAR

1 Complete the sentences with one of the following verbs in its infinitive or -*ing* form.

come   fry   grab   hit   lie   move   run   slam

1 I felt someone _____ my arm.
2 I heard someone _____ about downstairs in the living room.
3 I noticed his hat _____ on the ground.
4 She heard something heavy _____ the ground with a thud.
5 I could hear some strange noises _____ from the laboratory.
6 I heard the door _____.
7 I could smell the fish _____ in the kitchen.
8 I saw them _____ towards the village.

2 Put the words in the right order and make sentences.

1 hearing/down/remembers/stairs/she/ running/someone/the.

_____

_____

2 they/prince/lived/in/had/the/belonged/ house/to/a/that.

_____

_____

3 last/should/he/stayed/at/home/not/have/ night.

_____

_____

4 an/it/did/because/not/not/rain/umbrella/ have/I/need/taken.

_____

_____

5 not/our/the/did/have/to/show/cards/ identity/we/at/frontier.

_____

_____

6 to/television/we/have/every/licence/buy/ a/year.

_____

_____

3 Cross out the mistakes and write the correct sentences underneath.

1 Every morning he would to wake up at dawn to feed the cattle.

_____

_____

2 We did used to leave for school at half past six.

_____

3 Did she used to say prayers in the morning at her school?

_____

_____

4 You must to ring me as soon as you arrive.

_____

5 He shouldn't call the police, it just caused more trouble than it solved.

_____

_____

6 You needn't brought your dictionary, there are already some here.

_____

_____

7 I am used to work in the evenings now, but it wasn't easy at first.

_____

_____

8 I remember meet her for the first time.

_____

4 Write sentences with I remember...

1 I got into trouble at school for climbing trees.
I remember _____

_____

2 I wore a grey and red uniform.

_____

3 The headmistress had a very loud voice.

_____

4 She punished my sister for laughing out loud in assembly.

_____

_____

5 She took us on a number of school outings.

_____

6 I was very sad when I left school.

_____

5 Tick (✓) the pairs of sentences which have a similar meaning.

1 a You mustn't park on the main road.
  b You aren't allowed to park on the main road.
2 a You should have bought the car before the price went up.
  b You needn't have bought the car before the price went up.

3 a We couldn't get a ticket for the early flight.
  b We weren't able to get a ticket for the early flight.
4 a We needn't have called the police.
  b We didn't need to call the police.
5 a The neighbours must have seen something.
  b The neighbours had to see something.
6 a You mustn't drive over sixty miles an hour.
  b You don't have to drive over sixty miles an hour.
7 a We're used to dealing with dangerous criminals.
  b We're accustomed to dealing with dangerous criminals.
8 a We would talk late into the night.
  b We got used to talking late into the night.

6 Complete with *can, can't, must, mustn't, could, couldn't, have to* or *don't have to*. In some cases there may be more than one possibility.

1 You _____ come with us if you want to.
2 You _____ come if you don't want to.
3 You _____ return your tax form by Friday 8th if you don't want to be fined.
4 What _____ I do? It all happened so fast and the robbers were armed.
5 You _____ drive on the left in Britain.
6 You _____ drive on the right in Britain.
7 You _____ make a noise. There's a class next door.
8 You _____ cross the frontier because your passport is out of date.
9 I _____ go with you tomorrow, I've got another appointment.
10 You _____ call a lawyer but it is advisable.
11 Women _____ vote in Britain until 1928.
12 You _____ do that! It's against the law.

7 Write a second sentence so that it has a similar meaning to the first sentence, using the words in brackets.

1 My friend and I lived in the same flat. (shared)

_____

2 We used to spend every free moment down on the beach. (would)

_____

_____

3 You aren't allowed to smoke in the dining area. (mustn't)

_____

4 It is no longer possible to hunt elephants because they are a protected species. (can't)

_____

_____

5 You can't drive until you are eighteen. (illegal)

_____

6 That book is mine. (belong)

_____

7 I advise you not to jump the queue. (shouldn't)

_____

8 You mustn't make noise in the library. (allowed)

_____

9 It wasn't necessary to take a gift, but she did. (needn't)

_____

10 He couldn't recognise the burglar. (able)

_____

8 Rewrite the sentences with *need* or a suitable modal verb. There may be more than one possibility.

1 It is forbidden to own a firearm without a licence.

_____

_____

2 You made a statement to the police. It wasn't a good idea.

_____

_____

3 It wasn't possible to stop the thief because he was armed and I didn't have a gun.

_____

_____

4 You brought a tent but it wasn't necessary because they were provided.

_____

_____

5 You weren't expected to bring anything but the cake was very welcome.

_____

_____

6 Don't smoke here. It's prohibited.

_____

9 Complete the sentences with a suitable modal verb. There may be more than one possibility.

1 You are lucky to be alive! You _____ (take) such a risk. You _____ (be) shot.

2 Thank you very much indeed! You _____ (not, bring) anything. That's really very kind of you.

3 You _____ (take) a sleeping bag, because they are provided, but you _____ (forget) your backpack because there aren't enough for everyone.

4 We've just received a telegram saying that we _____ (move out) of the house at the end of the month. They are going to pull it down and build offices.

5 You _____ do that! It's against the law.

6 You _____ (see) the play this evening because it's not on. You _____ (go) tomorrow instead.

WRITING

1 Complete the sentences with phrases about you.

1 When I was at school I used to _____

_____ .

2 I can't get used to _____

_____ .

3 It didn't take me long to get used to _____

_____ .

4 I am used to _____

_____ .

5 There didn't use to be _____

at my school. _____

6 I wish I could get used to _____

_____ .

2 Look at the adjectives which describe emotions in *Vocabulary* activity 10. Choose five or six of these adjectives and for each one think of an incident which caused you to feel these emotions.
For each incident, write a few lines describing the situation and explaining your feelings.

3 Use one of the incidents in activity 1 as the basis for a story. You can develop the story in any way you wish by:

- inventing additional information
- describing the setting
- focusing on feelings

Try to include:

- a variety of past tenses
- participle clauses for dramatic effect
- linking words

4 Are the following offences a major problem in your country? What is the law about each of them?

- burglary
- mugging
- juvenile offenders
- owning weapons

5 Choose one of the problems in activity 4 and write a short essay giving your opinions.

Do you think present laws are satisfactory? If not, how could they be improved?

Lessons 11–13

VOCABULARY

1 Match a word on the left with a word on the right which has the opposite meaning.

1	odd	a	cooked
2	drawback	b	release
3	fresh	c	nearby
4	tender	d	gentle
5	raw	e	exposed
6	flaw	f	tough
7	steep	g	stale
8	remote	h	advantage
9	sheltered	i	normal
10	capture	j	quality

2 Complete the sentences below with words from activity 1. You may have to change the form of some of the words.

1 He was finally _____ last week after serving a four-year prison sentence for theft.

2 The lighthouse was in a very _____ place on the cliff top of an island in the Atlantic Ocean.

3 They thoroughly enjoyed their meal. The meat was _____ and the vegetables were exquisitely cooked.

4 The main _____ with cooking food in a car engine is the unpleasant smell.

5 I've got some _____ bread we can give to the ducks.

6 The main _____ in his character was his bad-temper.

7 We found a pleasant picnic spot, _____ from the wind.

8 The slope was so _____ they were out of breath when they got to the top.

3 Use a prefix to write the opposite or the negative of these words.

agree	_____	advantage	_____
connect	_____	typical	_____
usual	_____	appear	_____
suitable	_____	able	_____
convenient	_____	appropriate	_____
patient	_____	approve	_____
true	_____	legal	_____
qualify	_____	justice	_____
reputable	_____	practical	_____

4 Match the two parts of the sentences.

1 Take an umbrella ☐

2 Boil fresh milk ☐

3 Install a burglar alarm ☐

4 Take an aspirin ☐

5 Leave your car at home ☐

6 They had to work hard ☐

7 He bought a video ☐

8 I took a thick jacket ☐

9 Put vinegar on a wasp sting ☐

10 Never wear new shoes on a long hike ☐

a to relieve pain.

b to prevent it from swelling.

c in order to keep it longer.

d to keep their building company going.

e so that you don't get wet.

f to protect myself from the biting wind.

g in order not to get blisters.

h to keep thieves out.

i so he could record his favourite programmes.

j in order to avoid polluting the environment.

5 Match one of the following words with the descriptions 1–10 below. There are five extra words.

alarm   broom   fan   fax machine   foil
fork   fridge   hammer   kettle   ladle
microwave oven   saddle   saw   spade
spanner

1 It's for making horse riding
   more comfortable.   _____

2 It's for boiling water.   _____

3 You use it for digging the
   garden.   _____

4 It's a thing for serving soup.   _____

5 You can use it to wrap food
   in for oven-cooking.   _____

6 It's an appliance for cooking
   things quickly.   _____

7 It's a device for frightening
   burglars away.   _____

8 You use it to cut wood with.   _____

9 You use it to keep yourself
   cool in hot weather.   _____

10 It's used for keeping food
   cold.   _____

6 Describe the purpose of the extra words in activity 5.

1 _____

2 _____

3 _____

4 _____

5 _____

7 Combine the words in A with the words in B to form new words.

A	**B**
foot finger gun	work print mower
card shop sauce	brush board lifting
tooth house lawn	wood bin driver
screw dust fire	powder path pan

8 Write definitions for five of the new words in activity 7.

1 _____

2 _____

3 _____

4 _____

5 _____

9 Complete the series of words 1–12 with one of the following words.

chop   cream   dustpan   fax machine
hammer   oven   roast   sieve   smooth
swelling   tomato   wash

1 spanner   drill   nail   chisel _____

2 toaster   microwave   electric grill
   food processor _____

3 peeler   grater   whisk   strainer _____

4 mop   broom   bucket   cloth _____

5 cut   dice   slice   grind _____

6 fry   boil   bake   grill _____

7 aubergine   carrot   pepper   onion
   _____

8 stereo   video recorder   computer   radio
   _____

9 soft   tender   hard   rough _____

10 butter   milk   cheese   yoghurt
   _____

11 spot   bite   blister   sting _____

12 clean   wipe   rub   scrub _____

10 Use the words in brackets to form a word that fits in the space.

1 He accidentally hit himself with a hammer and his thumb is badly _____. (swell)

2 We've only got a third party _____ policy for our car because it's old and not worth very much. (insure)

3 It is hoped that genetical engineering will enable doctors to cure a number of _____ diseases in the future. (inherit)

4 Many of Francis Galton's _____ were impractical. (invent)

5 Every morning he used a metal _____ to look for money in the sand. (detect)

6 He tried to hide his _____. (disappoint)

7 She got a very bad mark in her maths test because of _____. (care)

8 It was such a _____ when she arrived home. We had been so worried. (relieve)

11 Complete the sentences.

1 That jug is too full. If you're not careful, you'll *s*_____ the milk.

2 She gave him the tablets and he *s*_____ them with a glass of water.

3 The dessert has a delicious creamy *t*_____ which the children like very much.

4 His computer caught a *v*_____ from a disk that came free with a magazine.

5 Her kitchen is equipped with a number of state-of-the-art electrical *a*_____.

6 You can change television channels by using the *r*_____ control.

12 Complete these phrasal verbs with the correct particle.

down   in   into   off   on   out   up

1 When he switched _____ the light, the bulb blew.

2 The burglar set _____ the alarm when he broke _____ the flat.

3 Everything in my home runs _____ electricity produced by solar energy.

4 All the electrical appliances were shut _____ by the main computer.

5 I have had a security alarm system put _____ because there have been a number of break-ins in the neighbourhood recently.

6 I have just taken _____ a new home insurance policy.

7 The computer company turned _____ to be incompetent.

8 The sales rep turned _____ at the door at a very inconvenient time.

9 I could never give _____ cheese. I like it too much.

10 He turned _____ a second helping because he had eaten enough.

13 Finish the sentences.

1 It was complicated_____.

2 It was unfair_____.

3 It is normal_____.

4 It was wrong_____.

5 It was generous_____.

6 It was clever_____.

GRAMMAR

1 Complete these sentences with *in order to, to* or *so (that)*.

1 We went into the department store
_____ buy a microwave.
2 I had a satellite dish installed _____
I could receive foreign channels.
3 I had a security system installed at my office
_____ prevent burglaries.
4 He went on a diet _____ lose
weight.
5 He has got a remote control _____
he can change channels without getting up
off the couch.
6 The engineer came to his home
_____ check his computer for
viruses.
7 Spray your computer screen with this
anti-static aerosol _____ it doesn't
get covered in dust.
8 Stand on the wall _____ you can
see the procession going by.

2 Complete these sentences with *of, for* or *to*.

1 It was careless ____ her ____ drop the dish.
2 What is this thing ____? It's ____ grilling raw
meat at the table.
3 It was unusual ____ him to get there early
4 It's an electrical appliance ____ playing
CDs.
5 It's a device ____ preventing milk from
boiling over.
6 It's rude not ____ remove your hat when
you enter someone's home.
7 It was silly ____ them not ____ book.
8 It was strange ____ him not ____ let us
know he was going away.
9 It would be stupid ____ her not ____ accept
the promotion.
10 He's used ____ cleaning windows.

**3 Cross out the mistakes and write the correct
sentences underneath.**

1 If I'll buy a new computer, I'll get connected
to e-mail.

_____

_____

2 I wouldn't be going to that restaurant unless
we really enjoy spicy food.

_____

_____

3 We go to the cinema tonight if we have
dinner early.

_____

_____

4 If I'm leaving this evening, I phone you
before five o'clock.

_____

_____

5 When I'm swimming in the sea, I will often
forget the time.

_____

_____

6 My house wouldn't be so untidy if I'd spend
more time at home.

_____

_____

7 When I'm going to the restaurant, I like to
eat something unusual.

_____

_____

8 If it's nice tomorrow, we have a barbecue.

_____

_____

4 Complete the sentences with the verbs in brackets in the correct form.

1 If I _____ (have to) go on a diet, I wouldn't give up eating cheese.

2 If I _____ (have) time at the weekend, I do the housework.

3 I'll meet you at the pub if I _____ (finish) work early this evening.

4 Put a thick coat on, otherwise you _____ (catch) a cold.

5 If you _____ (not hurry), we _____ (be) late for the performance.

6 I'm a vegetarian. I _____ (not, eat) raw meat even if I _____ (be) starving.

7 The bread _____ (go) stale if you _____ (not eat) it quickly.

8 If you _____ (not turn down) the heat, the milk _____ (boil over).

5 Complete the sentences with the best word or phrase: a, b, c or d.

1 It was very kind _____ him to stop and give us a lift.
   a for b of c to d as

2 It is important _____ him to pass the exam and go to university.
   a for b of c to d by

3 In order _____ be late, she took a taxi.
   a to not b so as not c so that d not to

4 I wouldn't go _____ I didn't have anything else to do. It just doesn't interest me.
   a unless b provided c even if
   d as long as

5 I'll lend you the money _____ you pay it back by the end of the month.
   a even if b as long as c unless
   d otherwise

6 The driveway is covered _____ a thick layer of snow.
   a with b by c for d under

7 The alarm was installed _____ a reputable security company _____ South London.
   a with, at b by, from c for, to d from, in

8 I won't come _____ you promise to let me drive.
   a if b provided c otherwise d unless

9 It is common _____ women _____ trousers to work nowadays.
   a of, to wear b of, to wear c for, to wear
   d for, wearing

10 _____ we aren't there by half past seven, don't wait for us.
    a unless b if c when d provided

6 Complete the sentences.

1 If I could speak _____

   _____.

2 I'll visit the USA if _____

   _____.

3 I won't get a good job unless _____

   _____.

4 They'll pass their exams as long as _____

   _____.

5 Work hard at school and university,
   otherwise _____

   _____.

6 Eat healthy food and take regular exercise if

   _____

   _____.

7 When I go to a restaurant, I _____

   _____.

8 I would find it difficult to give up _____

   _____.

9 I would go on a diet if _____

_____ .

10 When I eat too much, I _____

_____ .

7 **Complete the sentences in the correct form using the verbs in brackets.**

1 Our services _____ (present) in this brochure.

2 The system _____ (upgrade) this week.

3 Our video recorder and television _____ (both, damage) by a power surge last week.

4 The security system at the gallery _____ (change) since it _____ (break into) last month and a number of paintings _____ (steal).

5 Progress _____ (make) over the last decade in the treatment of a number of genetically linked diseases.

6 School children _____ (teach) to use computers in most schools.

7 The village _____ (flood) when the river rose after the heavy rainfall.

8 Police hope that the paintings _____ (recover) in the next few weeks.

8 **Rewrite these sentences in the passive.**

1 A company installed five new computers in our office yesterday.

_____

_____ .

2 Someone will check our computer network for viruses next week.

_____

_____ .

3 They didn't detect the flaw in the computer network in time.

_____

_____ .

4 Someone delivered the new photocopier this morning.

_____

_____ .

5 Dentists screen schoolchildren for dental problems twice a year.

_____

_____ .

6 The judge sentenced the man to five years in prison.

_____

_____ .

7 I think they should install computers in all classrooms.

_____

_____ .

8 I don't think they should censor the Internet.

_____

_____ .

WRITING

1 **Each of the following situations describes a decision or a judgment. For each one, make a list of words and sentences you could use to express your feelings and opinions. Here are some questions to help you.**

- Which judgments or decisions do you agree with and which do you disagree with?
- What is the general opinion?
- Is the judgement decision fair/practical?

35

- What effects will it have? Are these likely to be good, bad or of no account?
- What other implications are there?

Situation 1

In the 1960s a group of men committed one of the biggest robberies of all time. One of the men escaped to South America and has lived there peacefully and publicly ever since. Today, nearly thirty years later, extradition agreements have been signed between the two countries. The British government has decided to have the robber extradited so that he can finally stand trial and go to prison.

Situation 2

A well-known show business personality has been caught for tax evasion. He has deliberately cheated the state of over $250,000 in the last three years. He was fined $10,000 and ordered to pay his tax arrears.

Situation 3

An unemployed mother of three children was convicted of shoplifting for the third time in an out-of-town store. She was sentenced to three months in prison and her children were put into care.

2 You are going to write a letter to a newspaper giving your opinion about one of the situations in activity 1. Look back at your notes for ideas.

- first of all, explain why you are writing.
- say what you disagree with.
- explain why you disagree: give details and examples.
- say what you think would be a better judgment/decision.
- summarise your main points in the conclusion.

Here are some expressions you may find useful:

- I am writing to you because …
- In my opinion/view …
- An example of this is …
- That is a good point, but …
- It is true that …
- Nevertheless, …
- Many people believe/say …
- However, …
- In addition, we should consider …
- Not only but …
- Compared with …
- One advantage of this is/would be …
- An important difference to make is …
- In conclusion, I feel …

3 Look at the following aspects of travel and write down words and sentences you could use to talk about them under the headings.

Money	Health	Local customs
————	————	————
————	————	————
————	————	————
————	————	————
————	————	————

4 You are going to write a short article for a newspaper giving travel tips. For one or more of the topics in activity 3, write down tips and advice for travellers. Don't forget to explain your reasons and the possible consequences if they don't follow your advice.

Lessons 13-15

VOCABULARY

1 Use suffixes to make adjectives from these nouns and verbs.

custom _____   ancestor _____

health _____   farm _____

recognise _____   educate _____

faith _____   tradition _____

remark _____   benefit _____

memory _____   materialist _____

wealth _____   power _____

ecstasy _____   enthusiast _____

fury _____   nerve _____

worry _____   delight _____

produce _____   stress _____

2 Complete the sentences with a word(s) from activity 1. You may need to change the form of the word(s). There may be more than one possibility.

1 My brother John, who is an _____ Internet surfer, has just moved house to make room for his new computers and accessories.

2 The new computer network, which was installed early this year, has been especially _____ to my department which has enormously improved its _____.

3 When yet another _____ surge damaged the computer system, he was absolutely _____ and called the electricity company to demand compensation.

4 I was very _____ when my friend didn't get home at the usual time.

5 He takes sleeping tablets because his new job is very _____. .

6 It isn't very _____ to spend all day in front of a computer screen and then all evening in front of a television screen.

7 I was _____ when my colleagues threw a leaving party for me.

8 Their _____ came from Ireland and their community still keeps a number of _____ alive.

3 Match the two parts of the sentences.

1 E-mail is a network   ☐

2 He doesn't like people   ☐

3 New York is the city   ☐

4 Half past five is the time   ☐

5 The company   ☐

6 Our American friends   ☐

a where the nightlife is the most exciting.

b which sent the fax apologised for the mistake.

c when most farmers get up.

d which allows computer users to communicate with each other.

e who phone him after ten o'clock at night.

f whose house we stayed at were away for a fortnight.

4 Complete the sentences with the best word: a, b, c or d.

1 The plane was _____ from Heathrow airport to Gatwick because of thick fog on the runway.
   a cancelled   b diverted   c moved
   d connected

2 My daughter was _____ in an accident on the freeway out of Los Angeles.
   a crashed   b participated   c involved
   d failed

3 The flight crew _____ to stay calm and reassure the passengers throughout the ordeal.
   a managed   b could   c succeeded
   d allowed

4 The driver had forgotten to _____ his seatbelt.

a put   b fasten   c tie   d attach

5 Would you do me a _____ ? Could you lend me some cash until tomorrow?

a tip   b kindness   c thrill   d favour

6 The show was _____. We couldn't stop laughing all evening.

a far-fetched   b bizarre   c hilarious
d amusing.

7 Disneyland is one of the most popular tourist _____ in the USA.

a stations   b resorts   c sites   d attractions

8 They were so _____ that they didn't even bother to put T-shirts on over their swimming costumes when they came in for lunch.

a formal   b laid-back   c eccentric   d fit

9 In a truly democratic country the media are not _____.

a governed   b interpreted   c checked
d censored

10 We live in a _____ society where money and appearances are all important.

a tense   b materialistic   c anti-conformist
d cosmopolitan

5 Put the words you can use to describe a person's feelings and behaviour under the correct headings. There are five extra words.

far-fetched   distraught   thrilled   racist   upset
grateful   elegant   fortunate   nervous   bizarre
boring   fed-up   wealthy   frustrated
uneventful   pathetic   inspired   fascinating
eccentric   peculiar

Feelings	**Behaviour**
_____	_____
_____	_____
_____	_____
_____	_____
_____	_____
_____	_____
_____	_____
_____	_____

6 Complete the definitions with words from activity 5.

1 A story which is difficult to believe is _____.

2 A day when nothing special happens is _____.

3 Someone who has a lot of money is _____.

4 Someone who dresses smartly is _____.

5 Something which is not at all interesting is _____.

6 Someone who appreciates what another has done is _____.

7 Match a word on the left with a word on the right which has a similar meaning.

1	hurtle	a	laid-back
2	raise	b	distracted
3	massive	c	collect up
4	charming	d	possessions
5	pace	e	worried
6	distraught	f	lift
7	belongings	g	throw
8	gather	h	huge
9	relaxed	i	odd
10	anxious	j	delightful
11	peculiar	k	speed

8 Write a second sentence so that it has a similar meaning to the first sentence using the words in the brackets.

1 The early pioneers from Europe settled on the east coast. (established)

_____

_____

2 They were wearing the traditional Amish costume. (dressed)

_____

_____

3 Visitors are requested to take their shoes off and wash their feet before they enter the sacred building. (prior)

_____

_____

4 Cars and motorbikes are not allowed in the town centre. (banned)

_____

_____

5 You cannot replace the hand-written letter for personal mail. (substitute)

_____

_____

6 What is the purpose of being connected to e-mail? (point)

_____

_____

7 You can easily tell they are Amish from their unusual dress. (recognisable)

_____

_____

8 I went to the office to get my laptop computer. (fetch)

_____

_____

9 She's going to the airport now. (way)

_____

10 I wish I hadn't behaved so badly. (only)

_____

9 Write short definitions of these words.

dialect baptism jug hymn limousine vineyard windscreen ritual

1 _____

2 _____

3 _____

4 _____

5 _____

6 _____

7 _____

8 _____

GRAMMAR

1 Complete these sentences by putting the verb in brackets in a suitable passive.

1 The secretaries _____ (teach) how to use e-mail this morning.
2 They must _____ (show) how to store information on a disk.
3 Satellite viewers will _____ (give) access to more television channels.
4 Many people are worried about _____ (overhear) when they phone from public call boxes.
5 _____ (connect) to the Internet is great fun but very time-consuming.
6 _____ (contact) over the phone by advertising agencies is very annoying.
7 Many people approve of the idea of the Internet _____ (censor).
8 Many people are not aware of _____ (target) by advertisements.

2 Complete these sentences in the passive.

1 He has asked the company to disconnect his phone.
He has asked for_____

_____.

2 He likes people sending him e-mails rather than letters.
He likes to_____

_____.

3 Her software needs upgrading.
Her software needs_____

_____.

4 The company are checking his computer for viruses.
His computer_____

_____.

5 I've taken the car to the garage and someone is mending it.
I've taken the car to the garage _____

_____.

6 They must inform the staff of the company reorganisation plan.
The staff_____

_____.

7 They should introduce new laws to protect consumers.
New laws_____

_____.

8 He's worried about people faxing him a lot of junk-mail.
He's worried about_____

_____.

3 Complete the sentences with a suitable relative pronoun.

1 How old are the children _____ are in your afternoon class?
2 The student _____ room I have been sharing this term has left the course.
3 I got on the bus, _____ moved off immediately.
4 The person _____ sent me an e-mail is an old friend.
5 The office _____ I work now is very pleasant and spacious.
6 There's a lot of woodland _____ belongs to a wealthy farmer.
7 They work in the summer holidays, _____ helps their parents pay for their education.
8 The people _____ home we stayed at belong to the Amish community.

4 Put a tick (✓) by the sentences which have a defining relative clause and a cross (✗) by the sentence which have a non-defining relative clause.

1 The Americans who we met on a holiday have become close friends. ☐

2 The concert, which starts at nine o'clock, lasts for nearly three hours. ☐

3 I knocked on the front door, which was opened immediately. ☐

4 The people whose car we borrowed are our best friends. ☐

5 The flat where I live is on the sixth floor of a modern building. ☐

6 I left work late, which meant that I missed my train. ☐

7 Do you remember the time when we went to that ceremony? ☐

8 The man, who is driving the buggy, is a senior member of the community. ☐

5 Rewrite these sentences using participle clauses.

1 The family who lives next door comes from Poland.

_____

_____

2 The computers which control the space station are very old and keep breaking down.

_____

_____

3 I worked in a furniture shop which was situated on the main road into town.

_____

_____

4 We wrote a letter which explained our reasons for cancelling the meeting.

_____

_____

5 I have never met the people who work for the company.

_____

_____

6 Rewrite the sentences without *where*.

1 The place where I work is in the centre of town.

_____

2 The hotel where she is staying is by the sea.

_____

3 The flat where I live is on the second floor.

_____

4 The place where he goes at the weekend is near London.

_____

_____

7 Match the two parts of the sentences.

1 If I hadn't braked in time ☐
2 If only ☐
3 If it hadn't been delayed ☐
4 She would have passed her test ☐
5 I wish I knew ☐
6 If they hadn't complained ☐

a if she hadn't run into the police car.

b I wouldn't have missed my connection.

c how to work this thing.

d they hadn't lost the key.

e the management wouldn't have done anything.

f I'd have run the child over.

41

8 There is a mistake in each of these sentences. Cross out the mistake and write the correct sentences underneath.

1 The person came to the office this morning was a salesman.

_____

2 The house where my friends live in, is on the outskirts of town.

_____

3 She's worried about being charged much.

_____

4 The media shouldn't being censored.

_____

5 She's the fashion writer who articles I find so interesting.

_____

6 If she hasn't been delayed, she wouldn't have missed her train.

_____

7 He could been hurt badly if you hadn't intervened.

_____

8 If only I phoned my mother last week this wouldn't have happened.

_____

9 It sounds as if you had a good time. I wish I went with you.

_____

10 I wish I can get a better-paid job.

_____

9 For each situation write two sentences. One in the third conditional and one expressing regret.

1 I bought a small snake from the pet shop. The shop assistant said it was harmless. One day it escaped from its cage and bit the cat which died within the hour.

If it hadn't _____

_____ .

I wish _____

_____ .

2 I received a visit from someone claiming to be from the telephone company. He said that there was a problem with my line and asked to see the phone. The following night my house was burgled and electrical goods were taken. The burglar had climbed through the window which had been unlocked.

I wouldn't _____

_____ .

I should _____

_____ .

3 I had a bad experience when I travelled in a small two-seater plane in Africa. Since then I have been too frightened to fly again which is unfortunate because I love travelling.

If I hadn't _____

_____ .

If only _____

_____ .

4 I was driving to the garage to get my car tyres changed when I was stopped by a police car for speeding. The officer noticed my bald tyres and gave me a fine for that too.

I wouldn't_____

_____ .

I shouldn't_____

_____ .

WRITING

1 Write about a traditional lifestyle in your country. Make a list of words and expressions you could use to describe the way people live. Here are some questions to help you.

- Do many people live like this today?
- Is it mainly a rural or an urban way of life?
- Is the family very important?
- Do people speak a dialect?
- Is there a community hierarchy?
- Are the younger generation attached to this lifestyle?

2 Write an essay on the statement: *All traditional lifestyles are doomed in the long term.*

3 What is your relationship with modern technology? Write a few lines in answer to these questions.

- Do advances in modern technology make you feel bewildered, excited or indifferent?
- What is your favourite electrical appliance? Explain why.
- Do you enjoy trying out new devices?
- Are you excited about modern methods of communication such as e-mail, the Internet or satellite TV?
- Do you keep yourself informed about new technology or do you trail behind?

4 Write down three regrets you have about the past. For each regret, write a sentence saying what would or wouldn't have happened if you had acted differently.

1_____

_____

_____

2_____

_____

_____

3_____

_____

_____

Lessons 16–18

VOCABULARY

1 Circle the odd-one-out.

1 write create invent compose perform
2 samba rock bass jazz blues
3 saxophone trumpet clarinet guitar trombone
4 hit disc single LP album
5 cool mellow popular melodious
6 symphony pianist concerto opera
7 biography diary rhythm novel
8 orchestra portrayal group band choir

2 The dialogue below takes place in a bank. Complete the dialogue with the following words. You may need to change the form of some of the words. You may need to use some words more than once.

cash commission credit card cheque note withdrawal exchange refundable amount currency transaction trip abroad withdrawal traveller's cheque

A I shall be travelling (1)_____ a lot over the next year and I'd like some advice on travel money, please.

B What countries will you be visiting?

A Mainly European countries but I shall be making a (2)_____ to South America in January.

B It's a good idea to have some foreign (3)_____ for use when you arrive. You may want to make a phone call or pay a taxi so it's useful to have some small denomination (4)_____. However, it isn't advisable to carry too much (5)_____ in case you lose it or it is stolen.

A What alternatives are there?

B All over Europe you can use your (6)_____ to withdraw cash and even pay for goods or services.

A Is there a (7)_____ on cash (8)_____?

B Yes, it's one per cent of the total (9)_____.

A What rate of (10)_____ will I get?

B The rate on the day your (11)_____ goes through.

A Can I pay by (12)_____?

B Only in Europe with a Eurocheque book and card. Otherwise, no.

A What happens if I lose my card?

B You should inform us immediately. But it is sensible to have some (13)_____. These are safer than (14)_____ because they are (15)_____.

3 Match a word on the left with a word on the right which has the opposite meaning.

1	wholesale	a	generous
2	genuine	b	luxury
3	selfish	c	minority
4	increase	d	tiny
5	frivolous	e	artificial
6	immense	f	retail
7	borrow	g	reduce
8	necessity	h	spend
9	majority	i	lend
10	save	j	serious

4 Complete the sentences with a word(s) from activity 3. You may need to change the form of the word(s).

1 They put all their _____ into a pension scheme.

2 The management are pleased because the new company policy has resulted in a considerable _____ in production costs and _____ profits.

3 People gave _____ to the charity fund.

4 Although it was time-consuming, it was an _____ satisfying task.

5 The _____ of the situation forced them to intervene immediately.

6 I'm glad you didn't say anything to her because it was quite _____ and would only have hurt her feelings.

7 Perfume is a _____ which I indulge myself in occasionally.

8 I really don't like _____ flowers. They are not at all like the real thing.

5 Match the verbs with the phrases to form expressions.

break   come   do   get   let   look   make
put   run   set   take

1 _____ your breath away
2 _____ someone down
3 _____ a mistake
4 _____ your foot down
5 _____ a business
6 _____ a good example
7 _____ care of
8 _____ your heart
9 _____ rid of
10 _____ ends meet
11 _____ on the bright side
12 _____ a fuss
13 _____ two and two together
14 _____ for granted

15 _____ your own back on someone
16 _____ fire to
17 _____ off to a good start
18 _____ your best
19 _____ advantage of
20 _____ to your senses

6 Complete the sentences using an expression from activity 5. You may have to change some words.

1 He said she could rent the flat but at the last minute he changed his mind. She was very disappointed.
He _____ at the last minute.

2 When he went to live in Africa he realised that he missed a number of things he had never paid much attention to back home.
He missed things he had always _____ back home.

3 They paid such a lot of attention to her that she felt like a princess.
They _____ that she felt like a princess.

4 He was distraught with grief when his mother died.
His mother's death _____ .

5 She got her revenge on her employers by taking them to court and claiming compensation.
She _____ on her employers by taking them to court and claiming compensation.

6 She worked as hard as she could but she still failed the exam.
Even though she _____ , she still failed the exam.

7 He is the boss of an industrial cleaning firm.
He _____ which specialises in industrial cleaning.

8 I shall sell the car before it gets too old and unreliable.
I shall _____ before it gets too old and unreliable.

7 Complete the sentences with one of the following particles.

away   away with   down   for   into   off
out of   up   up with   without

1 We have run _____ an enormous bill at the grocer's which we will have to pay before the end of the month.
2 I really can't put _____ my job any longer. I'll have to look _____ another one.
3 I ran _____ petrol on the motorway and was towed off.
4 Burglars broke _____the flat in the early hours of the morning. They got _____ five thousand pounds worth of jewellery.
5 I hadn't seen her for over a year when she suddenly turned _____ last Monday.
6 They came _____ a wonderful plan to raise money.
7 He was so angry he tore _____ the report and threw it _____.
8 When you take notes, only write _____ the main points.
9 They set _____ at dawn because they had a long journey ahead of them.
10 I can do _____ my car in the city but not when I go _____ at weekends.

8 Complete these phrases with a suitable word.

1 a loaf of _____
2 a bottle of _____
3 a tube of _____
4 a can of _____
5 a bunch of _____
6 a dozen _____
7 a set of _____
8 an item of _____
9 a piece of _____
10 a pair of _____
11 a packet of _____
12 a box of _____
13 a tin of _____
14 a slice of _____

9 Complete the sentences with the best word: a, b, c or d.

1 It is essential that we find new ways to _____ energy.
a compose   b conserve   c combine
d contribute
2 The widespread use of fossil fuels which _____ carbon dioxide are the main cause of global warming.
a relieve   b reduce   c retain   d release
3 I listen to a lot of classical music because it has a _____ effect on my nerves.
a soothing   b softening   c harmonious
d mellow
4 A high _____ of the population live below the poverty line.
a production   b increase   c proportion
d variety
5 He received a letter from the bank informing him that his _____ was overdrawn.
a deposit   b loan   c mortgage   d account
6 I receive my bank _____ at the end of each month.
a statement   b interest   c withdrawal
d receipt
7 The school received a government _____ to pay for computer equipment.
a fee   b grant   c deposit   d tax
8 If the number of people out of work doesn't decrease, it will become difficult to _____ unemployment benefit for eveyone.
a promote   b provide   c complete
d exploit

10 Replace the underlined verbs with a suitable phrasal verb.

1 She <u>requested</u> an interview with the manager. _____

2 They <u>postponed</u> the meeting until the following week. _____

3 He <u>refused</u> their offer of help. _____

4 He <u>introduced</u> the pay issue at the beginning of the meeting. _____

5 It took them a long time to <u>recover</u> from the shock. _____

GRAMMAR

1 Rewrite the sentences replacing the word underlined with a pronoun.

1 Why did you tear up <u>the report</u>?

_____

2 I turned down <u>the offer of a job abroad</u>.

_____

3 He made up <u>the story</u> as he was telling it.

_____

4 He said he would pay back <u>the money</u> at the end of the month.

_____

5 Would you turn off <u>the music</u>, please?

_____

6 She brought up <u>the financial issue</u> at the last meeting.

_____

2 Tick (✓) the sentences where the underlined word is an uncountable noun.

1 What is the <u>weather</u> going to be like? ☐

2 Just tell him that it's none of his <u>business</u>. ☐

3 He has just started up a new software <u>business</u>. ☐

4 <u>Jazz</u> is my favourite type of music. ☐

5 We had a lot of <u>fun</u> at the party. ☐

6 I go to the <u>market</u> twice a week. ☐

7 The removals van came and started loading our <u>furniture</u>. ☐

8 The <u>bulk</u> of our commercial deals are with European countries. ☐

9 We had a good <u>journey</u> home. ☐

10 We won't have <u>time</u> for any more questions, I'm afraid. ☐

11 I wish I could afford better <u>accommodation</u>. ☐

12 Could I have a <u>receipt</u>, please? ☐

13 Can you get some <u>fruit</u> from the shops, please? ☐

14 They produce <u>rubber</u> in Malaysia. ☐

15 Everything is covered in <u>dust</u>! ☐

16 Could you lend me some <u>cash</u> until tomorrow, please? ☐

3 Put a tick (✓) by the pairs of sentences which have a similar meaning

1 a There were quite a few people at the performance. ☐
  b There were quite a lot of people at the performance.

2 a I've got hardly any cash left. ☐
  b I haven't got much cash left.

3 a There were few new faces at the party. ☐
  b There were a few new faces at the party.

4 a I hope we will pay less tax. ☐

   b I hope we will only pay a little
      tax.

5 a There's none left. ☐

   b There isn't any left.

6 a There are few people who ☐
      would admit to that.

   b There aren't many people who
      would admit to that.

4 Cross out the mistakes and write the correct sentences underneath.

1 We don't need many time to repair the car.

   _____

2 I've only got little foreign currency left.

   _____

3 When you go to the shop, can you get me any bottles of water, please?

   _____

4 There's a quite lot of interest in their new album.

   _____

5 There's not much of money left in my account.

   _____

6 I haven't got great deal of time today.

   _____

7 There were quite few spectators at the match.

   _____

8 I'd like dozen eggs, please and a couple ripe melons.

   _____

9 I haven't got enough of money to pay my electricity bill.

   _____

10 There is several explanations for their peculiar behaviour.

   _____

5 Complete the sentences with a suitable expression of quantity.

any   a few   enough   hardly   little   more
much   some

1 I've got _____ money to pay the milkman but not the garage.

2 There are quite _____ dealers interested in buying the portrait.

3 There are a lot _____ tourists here this year.

4 There is _____ anything in the fridge.

5 Can I have _____ more coffee, please?

6 You can buy it from _____ chemist shop.

7 There's very _____ that I can do to help you, I'm afraid.

8 How _____ is the painting worth, would you say?

6 Choose the best verb tense.

1 I *will go/will be going* to the conference on crime next week in Brussels.

2 I doubt if I *will be finishing/will have finished* it by next Thursday. I'll *need/be needing* more time.

3 The proportion of unemployed *will increase/will have increased* dramatically by the end of the decade if something isn't done.

4 Fifty years from now, we will almost certainly *live/be living* in a better world.

5 I don't think the balance of power in the world *will be changing/will have changed* much by the end of the next decade.

6 I hope we *will move/will be moving* into our new flat at the end of the month.

7 Rewrite the sentences using the future perfect or the future continuous and the verb in brackets.

1 The government has approved a massive grant to equip all primary school classrooms with computers by the end of the decade. By the end of the decade, all primary schoolchildren (use) _____.

2 There is a seminar on language teaching next month. I have taken the week off work to go.
I (attend) _____.

3 Their plane was at eleven o'clock. It's twelve thirty now.
They (take off) _____.

4 The numbers of many animal species decrease every year and this trend is likely to continue.
In twenty years time many species (disappear) _____.

8 Complete the passage with these words and expressions.

Amazingly   In conclusion   In fact
In my experience   In my opinion
Personally   To my mind   Unfortunately

(1)_____, I am resolutely optimistic about the future of mankind. (2)_____, the present atmosphere of pessimism is totally unjustifiable. (3)_____, when a group of people talk about the environment or future trends in society, they immediately start by presenting the worst possible scenarios as if there were no alternatives. (4)_____, there are alternatives if only we would look for them. (5)_____, the people who have the gloomiest outlook are very often those who have an excellent standard of living. (6)_____, we should look to the extraordinary advances being made in science and technology for the answers to our problems. (7)_____, many people see them as the principle cause of many of society's troubles. (8)_____, what is needed is a positive and determined approach to society's problems rather than the defeatist-at-the-outset attitude which is too often the case.

WRITING

1 Write a review of a film or a television programme you have seen recently. Choose something which you either enjoyed very much or didn't like at all.
Describe it briefly and say why you liked/disliked it.

2 Answer the questions about a shopping outing you have been on recently.

- when was it?
- where did you go?
- what did you intend to buy?
- what did you buy?
- who did you buy things for?
- did you enjoy yourself?
- did you do anything you hadn't planned?
- did anything unexpected happen to you?

3 Use the questions in activity 2 to help you write a paragraph about a shopping outing.

4 Read the passage in *Grammar* activity 8 again. What would be a good title for this passage? Do you agree with the views of the writer? Write a paragraph giving your opinion.

Lessons 18–20

VOCABULARY

1 Replace the underlined words with a suitable phrasal verb from the list below. In some cases, you may have to rewrite the sentence.

break down   break into   carry on
get away with   hand out   let down
run out of   set out   stand for

1 I shouldn't take any notice of what they say. Just <u>continue</u> doing things the way you want to.

_____

2 Three men <u>entered</u> our house last night and <u>stole</u> all the family silver.

_____

3 The washing machine <u>stopped working</u> just when we needed it most.

_____

4 In many people's minds, Rolls Royce <u>represents</u> both quality and luxury.

_____

5 I recommend that brand of washing machine. It <u>is very reliable</u>.

_____

6 They walked around the city centre <u>distributing</u> leaflets.

_____

7 <u>Their intention was</u> to shock people with their outrageous advertisements.

_____

8 I'm sorry, we haven<u>'t any more</u> tea.

_____

2 Put the words below under the correct heading.

battle bells bravery castle ceremony
chivalry cliffs church coast drown float
harbour king knight legend mainland
medieval monastery saint sink spire
sword temple tide wave worship wreck

Past times	The sea	Christianity
_____	_____	_____
_____	_____	_____
_____	_____	_____
_____	_____	_____
_____	_____	_____
_____	_____	_____
_____	_____	_____
_____	_____	_____
_____	_____	_____
_____	_____	_____

3 Add more words to the groups in activity 2. You can use your dictionary.

4 Match these definitions with a word from activity 2.

1 A hereditary leader. _____
2 The regular movement of the ocean. _____
3 The remains of a ship. _____
4 An ancient weapon. _____
5 A religious retreat for men. _____
6 The social code of bravery and courtesy in medieval times. _____
7 A holy person. _____
8 To die in water. _____

5 Complete the sentences.

1 In their election manifesto the Conservatives said they would increase Government *s*_____ on education.

2 Since they have been in power they have *c*_____ over two thousand jobs in the public sector.

3 During elections most political parties promise to *r*_____ income tax but when they are in power they invariably *i*_____ it!

4 Nurses are going on strike because they say that most hospitals are *u*_____ and they are obliged to work very long hours.

5 They promised to *l*_____ the school-leaving age from seventeen to sixteen.

6 This Government is determined to *r*_____ interest rates so that more people can buy their own homes.

7 The Social Democrat party finally won the *e*_____ after being in *o*_____ for over eight years.

8 They are holding a *r*_____ on the issue of European currency.

6 Use a word in brackets to form a word that fits in the space.

1 Although the questions were _____ difficult, a high proportion of students passed the exam.   (relative)

2 She told me that it was a small, _____ family company.   (rely)

3 The drawing was an excellent _____ of the house but it had very little artistic value.   (represent)

4 Even as a child he had an extraordinary _____.   (image)

5 He suddenly _____ and nobody ever heard of him again.   (appear)

6 We took some time off for _____ at four o'clock.   (refresh)

7 Our company have spent a lot of money on

_____ and they expect it to increase sales considerably.   (advert)

8 The main advantage of that particular car is that it is very _____ on petrol.   (economy)

9 The figures show that car _____ are up this month for the first time in over a year.   (sell)

10 The key to a successful global advertisement is _____.   (simple)

11 It was most _____ of them to remember her birthday.   (consider)

12 He is very _____ about modern literature.   (know)

7 Circle the words you associate with advertising.

global   brand   trouble   sell   product
reliable   raft   image   appeal   increase
promote   international   message   alien
slogan   technique   maiden   campaign
quality   leisure   symbolise   surplus

8 Circle the verbs which describe noises people make.

creak   laugh   bark   scream   sing   ring
mutter   scrape   shout   buzz   groan
stammer   bang   whisper

9 Match the verbs in activity 8 with the situations.

1 You would do this when you find something funny.   _____

2 When you don't want to be overheard you do this.   _____

3 In a sudden frightening situation you may do this.   _____

4 If you want to attract someone's attention who is at a distance you may do this.   _____

5 If you are not pleased about something you may do this to yourself. _____

6 You may do this when you are asked to do something you don't want to. _____

10 Put a tick (✓) by the statements which are true for your country.

1 General elections are held every five years. ☐
2 The head of state is a president. ☐
3 The president is elected for life. ☐
4 In Parliament there are MPs who represent the different parties. ☐
5 The Prime Minister is the head of government. ☐
6 There is a strong opposition party. ☐
7 We never have referendums. ☐
8 Every citizen over the age of eighteen can vote. ☐
9 There is proportional representation in local government. ☐
10 The party in power changes regularly. ☐

11 Correct the statements in activity 10 which are not true for your country.

1 _____

2 _____

3 _____

4 _____

5 _____

6 _____

7 _____

8 _____

9 _____

10 _____

12 Complete the sentences with the best word: a, b, c or d.

1 The government said they were going to _____ smoking in all public buildings.
a stop b ban c remove d finish

2 A global advertisement has to have a simple _____ which can be easily translated.
a appeal b image c product d message

3 His _____ views on employment have made him unpopular with both politicians and union members.
a conflicting b contradicting
c controversial d competent

4 The nation's _____ balance was positive last year due to a spectacular increase in exports.
a trade b economic c tax d sales

5 The party lost its _____ in Parliament and elections had to be called.
a opposition b constituency c assembly
d majority

6 A massive tidal _____ swept the boat out to sea.
a raft b wave c log d wreck

7 There has been a general drop in the _____ of living over the last five years.
a record b level c standard d balance

8 He had a car accident but _____ he was not seriously injured.
a presumably b hopefully c actually
d fortunately

13 What products are these slogans for?

breakfast cereal   car   exercise bicycle
mobile phone   suitcase   toothpaste

1 THE GREATEST DRIVE IN THE WORLD

_____

2 GET A CRISPY CRUNCHY START TO THE
DAY

_____

3 TRAVEL IN STYLE WITH OUR NEW
EXECUTIVE RANGE

_____

4 FOR A SPARKLING SMILE USE VIMTO
EVERY DAY

_____

5 GET INTO OLYMPIC FORM IN YOUR OWN
HOME

_____

6 IT'S A SMALL WORLD AT A SMALL PRICE

_____

14 What do the slogans claim about the
products?

1 _____

2 _____

3 _____

4 _____

5 _____

6 _____

GRAMMAR

1 These sentences were election pledges.
When the party came to power they didn't
do any of the things they promised. Rewrite
the sentences using the future in the past.

1 We will take action to reduce urban
pollution.

They_____.

2 We will improve healthcare.

They_____.

3 We won't increase income tax.

They_____.

4 We will develop closer links with Europe.

They_____.

5 We won't reduce public spending on
defence.

They_____.

2 Match the two parts of the sentences.

1 He had warned them not ☐
2 She threatened ☐
3 I complained ☐
4 She apologised ☐
5 She asked ☐
6 He promised ☐
7 He pointed out ☐
8 We insisted ☐
9 I agreed ☐
10 He admitted ☐

a for her money back.

b to take her out to the restaurant of her
choice on her birthday.

c with them that there had been some
problems.

d to call the police if they didn't stop making a
noise.

e on paying the bill.

f for arriving late.

g that there was very little anyone could do to change the situation now.

h to driving carelessly but he said he had definitely not damaged the car.

i to buy the car, so they only had themselves to blame when it let them down.

j about the shower and they gave me another room.

3 Rewrite the main idea of these sentences in reported speech using one of the following verbs.

admit   advise   apologise   ask   complain
offer   suggest   warn

1 'I'm sorry I was out when you called this morning,' she said.

_____

_____

2 'I should lock all your doors and windows.' she said.

_____

_____

3 'Let's invite some friends over tomorrow evening,' he said.

_____

_____

4 'I bought this radio last week and it's already broken,' she said to the sales assistant.

_____

_____

5 'Don't walk so near the edge of the cliff, you might slip,' she said to her children.

_____

_____

6 'Can I have a receipt, please?' she asked.

_____

_____

7 'Would you like a lift into town, Peter?' she asked.

_____

_____

8 'I suppose I was a bit unfair with the children,' she said.

_____

_____

4 In each of these sentences there is a word missing. Put a cross where the word should be and write the missing word in the space.

1 She decided ask for a pay rise so she went to see her boss.   _____

2 What caused the Titanic sink in the Atlantic Ocean?   _____

3 Stonehenge can't have built from local stone because it is of a different type.   _____

4 It believed that Arthur was a Celtic leader of the 6th or 7th century.   _____

5 It was cold that they decided not to go out.   _____

6 They insisted taking the car into the town centre.   _____

7 They couldn't decide to buy a Mercedes or a Porsche.   _____

8 The car was sold to us a dishonest dealer.   _____

5 Write sentences drawing conclusions with the words in bold.

1 I'm sure it was Anna singing on the radio. It certainly sounded like her.
must

_____

_____

2 I thought I saw your father at the match on Saturday. But you say he was in hospital at the time.
can't

_____

_____

3 I'm not sure where they used to live but they have a slight Irish accent.
may

_____

_____

4 I'm not sure what he studied at university but he seems to know an awful lot about chemistry.
might

_____

_____

5 I heard my daughter crying in bed. When I went in to comfort her she had gone back to sleep.
must

_____

_____

6 Rewrite these sentences using a suitable passive construction and the verb in brackets.

1 This Government will do better than its predecessor. (hope)

_____

_____

2 Everyone agrees that they are the best team in the world. (acknowledge)

_____

_____

3 The Loch Ness monster is an enormous fish. (believe)

_____

_____

4 Archimedes discovered his famous theorem while having a bath. (allege)

_____

_____

5 Children who are good-mannered are seen and not heard. (consider)

_____

_____

6 Regular exercise is good for your health. (know)

_____

_____

7 Complete the passages with one of the following words or phrases.

as a result   definitely   fortunately   I suppose
in general   in my opinion   it is obvious
personally   presumably   on the contrary
in fact   of course

1 (1)_____, advertising should be banned from television altogether. (2)_____, I turn the set off when the adverts come on because I can't stand them. (3)_____, there are people who do watch them. I doubt if companies would pour so much money into advertising campaigns if they didn't help sell their products. (4)_____, there is one channel which has no advertising so I can watch that in peace.

2 (1)_____, I am quite unusual in that I really like watching the adverts on TV. (2)_____, I know a lot of adverts off by heart and I often find myself humming a tune from one when I'm working. (3)_____, I don't let adverts influence me when I buy something. (4)_____, I deliberately avoid products I've seen on the TV.

3 (1)_____, I think the Government should reduce income tax drastically. It is (2)_____ the only way to boost public confidence. (3)_____ that by maintaining high taxation the economy cannot take off. (4)_____, people have very little money to spend on consumer goods and (5)_____, high street sales have fallen and many shopkeepers have gone bankrupt.

WRITING

1 Answer these questions about advertising.

- Is there a lot of advertising on TV and radio in your country?
- Do you watch the adverts on TV or do you turn the TV off?
- In general, do you enjoy watching adverts?
- Can you think of any advertisements that you find particularly irritating?
- Do you believe that advertising has an influence on you? If so, what kind of influence?

2 Describe an advertisement that you found particularly striking.

_____

_____

_____

_____

_____

_____

_____

_____

_____

3 Choose a product and write your own radio advertisement.

Answer Key

Lessons 1–3

VOCABULARY

1   1 h   2 k   3 l   4 a   5 i   6 d   7 j   8 c   9 b
    10 f   11 e   12 g

2   1 deliberately   5 confessed
    2 fans   6 close
    3 rules   7 current
    4 smile, opponents   8 pitch

3   1 pinch   2 opportunity   3 kick   4 pitch   5 chew
    6 event   7 foreigner   8 perform

4   a pitch   b event   c chew   d foreigner   e pinch
    f kick   g opportunity   h perform

5   bow: back, body   point: finger
    chew: teeth   scratch: nails
    clap: hands   shrug: shoulders
    frown: forehead   stare: eyes
    grin: mouth, face   wave: hand
    kiss: lips, mouth   wink: eye
    nod: head   yawn: mouth
    pat: hand

6   2 e   3 a   4 j   5 i   6 h   7 b   8 f   9 c   10 g

7   **Verb:** address   attend   fail   gesture   kneel
    laugh   vary
    Adjective: awe-inspiring   deadly   electric
    frantic   forgivable   native   profitable   strict
    suspicious
    Noun: address   cheek   coincidence   commentary
    customs   gesture   heart   laugh   native

8   1 acceptable   5 behaviour   8 acquaintances
    2 insulting   6 rewarding   9 recognised
    3 childhood   7 spoken   10 profitable
    4 friendship

9   1 forward   2 expected   3 worried   4 opportunity
    5 address   6 codes   7 guess   8 forgotten

10 1 how   2 what   3 where   4 which   5 who
    6 when   7 why

11 1 Is it polite to stare at someone you don't know?
    2 Should you shake hands when you say
      goodbye?
    3 Have you ever made a social mistake?
    4 How do you greet close friends?
    5 Is it rude to blow your nose in public?
    6 Would you like to see a big football match?
    7 Is football popular with both men and women?
    8 Who won the last World Cup?

GRAMMAR

1   1 Have you ever been …
    2 … spoken English …
    3 Does he ever use …
    4 Who speaks to you most …
    5 Are you looking forward to …
    6 …, did you?
    7 Can you understand …
    8 … attended …
    9 Should you shake hands …
    10 Are there any …

3   *Example answers*
    1 How far is it from the centre of town?
    2 Let's go to the cinema, shall we?
    3 What's your new teacher like?
    4 Do you speak in your own language during
      lessons?
    5 Have you ever been to an English speaking
      country?
    6 How much time do you spend cycling?
    7 Do you think it is important to conform to social
      norms?
    8 Do children find it easier to learn a foreign
      language?
    9 How long does it take (to get here)?
    10 Did you go shopping yesterday?

4   1 the   8 an   15 the   22 a
    2 the   9 a   16 The   23 an
    3 a   10 a   17 the   24 a
    4 the   11 the   18 a   25 the
    5 the   12 a   19 the   26 the
    6 an   13 the   20 a
    7 a   14 the   21 a

5   1 shall we?   5 will you?   9 won't there
    2 Why don't   6 did you?   10 will you
    3 are you?   7 doesn't he?
    4 isn't it?   8 have you?

Lessons 3–5

VOCABULARY

1 **Theatre:** acting applaud audience stage
play scene performance company
Athletics: race applaud marathon winner
running lose jumping performance stadium
track final
Sightseeing: landmark guide museum visit
palace building

2 *Example answers*
Football: goal player score stadium team
Shopping: cash desk chain store clothing
department store sales assistant
Travelling by train: destination passenger
railway ticket track

3 1 football 2 fishing 3 watching television
4 politics 5 skiing 6 dancing

4 1 f 2 j 3 l 4 g 5 a 6 d 7 c 8 k 9 e
10 h 11 b 12 i

5 1 failure   7 accomplished
2 surroundings   8 celebrity
3 performance   9 triumphantly
4 boring   10 satisfaction
5 succesful   11 applause
6 actress   12 moving

6 1 c 2 b 3 d 4 a 5 a 6 d 7 b 8 c 9 b
10 c

7 1 We have enjoyed ourselves here this week.
2 He is always worrying about his job.
3 I gradually realised how fond I was of the
cottage.
4 Our new neighbours make a lot of noise.
5 I regret not having travelled more when I was
young and fit.
6 Seeing the sunset reminds me of the past.
7 He owes the bank a lot of money.
8 He was determined to resist temptation and
revise for his exam.

8 1 optimist 2 pessimist 3 graduate
4 self-confident 5 compromise 6 talented
7 determined 8 Failure

9 formal: 2 3 5 6 8 10

informal: 1 4 7 9

10 coastal   rainy
confused/confusing   rhythmic/rhythmical
deserted   sandy
determined   scenic
dusty   sleepy/sleepless
failing   steamy
faithful/faithless   successful
hazy   talented

mountainous   triumphant
optimistic   tropical
pounding   wealthy
profitable

GRAMMAR

1 1 (ask) to 2 ✓ 3 the 4 gone 5 ✓
6 to 7 to 8 to

2 1 How about   6 will
2 can/could   7 Shall
3 can/could   8 shall
4 will   9 Let's
5 why don't/couldn't 10 will

3 1 taken   7 Have you seen
2 have been standing   8 have you had
3 known   9 have you done
4 have been mending   10 haven't visited,
5 have only read   haven't had
6 have you been doing

4 1 c f 2 k n 3 e i 4 g 5 a l 6 m o 7 h j
8 b d

5 1 have made   5 have been thinking,
2 didn't know,   have decided
did you stay   6 Have you been sitting
3 has grown   7 has written
4 has been reading, 8 have you had
got

6 1 How long have you been living in this town?
2 How many new students have you met?
3 I haven't known the director very long.
4 They have been studying chemistry for four
years now.
5 How long have you been smoking?
6 How many cigarettes have you smoked today?
7 She's been working since eight o'clock.
8 What have you achieved in your life?

7 1 are going to   5 won't/will you
2 will   6 are going to, Will/Won't
3 will   7 will
4 are you going to   8 are you going to

8 *Example answers*
1 I'll drive very carefully.
2 I won't do the washing up.
3 Will you give me a lift into town?
4 Will/won't you stay and have a cup of tea?
5 I'll make the dinner.

Lessons 6–8

VOCABULARY

1 1 patient 2 prescription 3 hospital 4 hurt
   5 pill 6 accident 7 pain 8 anaesthetic
   9 emergency 10 ears

2 1 plaster 2 toothache 3 appointment
   4 sedative 5 prescription 6 outpatients
   7 disabled 8 disease 9 thermometer
   10 operations

3 **Long actions:** gaze hold listen observe
   peer squeeze stare stroke watch
   Short actions: glance glimpse grab grasp
   hit kick nod notice nudge pinch punch
   snatch

4 1 glanced 2 staring 3 gazing 4 glimpse
   5 grabbed 6 snatched 7 punched

5 1 a 2 d 3 c 4 b 5 c 6 b 7 a 8 d 9 a
   10 c 11 b 12 c

6 1 soundly 2 scrupulously 3 gratefully
   4 directly 5 cautiously 6 Impulsively
   7 successfully 8 Surprisingly 9 intentionally
   10 skilfully

8 1 suspected 2 sedative 3 burial 4 deception
   5 emptied 6 threatened, threat 7 disappointing
   8 confused 9 impression 10 disturbance

9 1 beach 2 jungle 3 stream 4 estuary
   5 footpath 6 peak 7 horizon 8 waterfall
   9 farmland 10 range 11 hedge 12 pass
   13 meadow 14 oasis 15 wood

10 crops farmland fertile harvest irrigation

GRAMMAR

1 1 Not wanting to upset her, I didn't mention the
     accident.
   2 Waking up early, I went out for a walk.
   3 Crossing the park, I noticed my friend sitting
     on a bench.
   4 Standing up suddenly, Sherlock walked to the
     window.
   5 We followed the footpath running along the
     top of the cliff.
   6 She spoke to the woman working in the
     garden.
   7 Not wanting to go shopping, I ordered a pizza
     to be delivered.
   8 Turning her head round slowly, she caught a
     glimpse of the ghost.

2 1 a six-year-old boy
   2 a two-hour journey
   3 a four-course dinner
   4 a three-hour film
   5 an eighteen-hole golf course
   6 a five-hundred-pound hotel room
   7 a ten-storey office block
   8 a four-bedroom house

3 1 There is an excellent, new visitor centre in
     Culloden.
   2 Loch Ness is a beautiful, long, narrow loch.
   3 Glencoe is a breathtakingly beautiful,
     windswept mountain pass.
   4 Portree is a popular, seaside tourist centre.
   5 Ben Nevis is an unattractive, 4,406 foot-high
     mountain which lies to the east of Fort
     William.
   6 There's a spectacular, two-hundred-year-old,
     ruined castle at the top of a cliff.
   7 There are wonderful, sheltered, sandy beaches.
   8 There is a row of picturesque, freshly painted,
     terraced houses above the harbour.

4 1 along 2 to 3 between 4 on 5 through
   6 in 7 by 8 on 9 past 10 by

5 1 had been, went
   2 were driving, stopped
   3 had been living, died
   4 had been walking, reached
   5 passed, had only been studying
   6 hasn't left, arrived
   7 got, had forgotten
   8 had been working
   9 had been waiting
   10 had been running, retired
   11 has been running
   12 had examined

6 1 After leaving college, I applied for a job.
   2 I remembered to order dinner before going
     out.
   3 After posting the letter, I went for a cup of
     coffee.
   4 After visiting my mother in the ward, I talked
     to the consultant.
   5 After studying for three years in York, he
     moved to London.
   6 He worked as a waiter for a year before going
     to live abroad.
   7 After having a heart attack, he stopped
     smoking.
   8 After finishing work, we went to the football
     match.

7   1 have ever held   13 arrived
    2 have never been   14 put
    3 had seen   15 were having/had
    4 had made   16 had been chatting
    5 took   17 remembered
    6 went   18 had left
    7 bought   19 had been cooking
    8 didn't look   20 was feeling
    9 had arrived   21 phoned
    10 bought   22 had been taken
    11 worked   23 had not had
    12 was still cooking 24 have not held

Lessons 8–10

VOCABULARY

1   1 d 2 f 3 j 4 a 5 h 6 k 7 l 8 c 9 e
    10 g 11 b 12 i

2   1 vacancy 2 suitable 3 forbidden 4 glamorous
    5 smelly 6 confession 7 permission
    8 hesitation 9 conviction 10 encouraging

3   **Light:** bright colour dark dim dingy
    gloomy see
    Sound: aloud bang clang creak deafening
    hum noisy ringing rustle thud tinkle
    tumult
    Touch: caress contact feel hard pat rough
    sticky stroke

4   1 hiccups 2 snoring 3 cried 4 creaked
    5 barking 6 groaned 7 whistled 8 rumble
    9 rustling 10 sniffing 11 thud 12 slammed
    13 gasped 14 sighed

5   1 a e g i k   2 d h   3 b j   4 c f

6   1 truth 2 weapon 3 innocent 4 bail 5 trial
    6 barrister

7   1 witness
    2 arson
    3 barrister/lawyer
    4 fine
    5 illegal/unlawful/prohibited
    6 burglar
    7 jury
    8 prosecute

8   1 convicted, sentenced
    2 judge/jury, guilty
    3 offence
    4 trial
    5 accused
    6 charges
    7 innocent
    8 law

9   1 e 2 f 3 d 4 b 5 a 6 c

10 *Example answers*
    1 astonished 2 frightened 3 incredulous
    4 inadequate 5 sympathetic 6 outraged
    7 hurt   8 proud

GRAMMAR

1   1 grab 2 moving 3 lying 4 hit 5 coming
    6 slam 7 frying 8 running

2   1 She remembers hearing someone running
      down the stairs.
    2 They lived in a house that had belonged to the
      prince.
    3 He should not have stayed at home last night.
    4 I need not have taken an umbrella because it
      did not rain.
    5 We did not have to show our identity cards at
      the frontier.
    6 We have to buy a television licence every year.

3   1 … he would wake up …
    2 We used to …
    3 Did she use to …
    4 You must ring me …
    5 He shouldn't have called …
    6 You needn't have brought …
    7 … to working
    8 … meeting her

4   1 I remember getting into trouble …
    2 I remember wearing …
    3 I remember the headmistress having …
    4 I remember her punishing …
    5 I remember her taking us on …
    6 I remember being very sad …

5   **Similar meaning:** 1 3 7
    Different meaning: 2 4 5 6 8

6   1 can   5 have to   9 can't
    2 don't have to 6 mustn't   10 don't have to
    3 must/have to   7 mustn't   11 couldn't
    4 could   8 can't   12 mustn't/can't

7   1 My friend and I shared a flat.
    2 We would spend …
    3 You mustn't smoke …
    4 You can't hunt elephants …
    5 It's illegal to drive …
    6 That book belongs to me.
    7 You shouldn't jump the queue.
    8 You aren't allowed to make a noise …
    9 You needn't have taken …
    10 He wasn't able to recognise …

8 *Example answers*
   1 You must have a licence to own a firearm.
   2 You shouldn't have made a statement to the police.
   3 I couldn't stop the thief because …
   4 You needn't have brought …
   5 You needn't have brought the cake.
   6 You mustn't smoke here.

9 1 shouldn't have taken, could have been
   2 didn't need to bring
   3 don't need to take, mustn't forget
   4 have to move out
   5 mustn't
   6 can't see, will have to go

Lessons 11–13

VOCABULARY

1 1 i 2 h 3 g 4 f 5 a 6 j 7 d 8 c
   9 e 10 b

2 1 released 2 remote 3 tender 4 drawback
   5 stale 6 flaw 7 sheltered 8 steep

3 disagree disconnect unusual unsuitable
   inconvenient impatient untrue disqualify
   disreputable disadvantage atypical disappear
   unable inappropriate disapprove illegal
   injustice impractical

4 1 e 2 c 3 h 4 a 5 j 6 d 7 i 8 f
   9 b 10 g

5 1 saddle 2 kettle 3 spade 4 ladle 5 foil
   6 microwave oven 7 alarm 8 saw 9 fan
   10 fridge

7 footprint footpath fingerprint gunpowder
   cardboard shoplifting saucepan toothbrush
   housework lawnmower screwdriver dustbin
   dustpan firewood

9 1 hammer 2 oven 3 sieve 4 dustpan 5 chop
   6 roast 7 tomato 8 fax machine 9 smooth
   10 cream 11 swelling 12 wash

10 1 swollen 2 insurance 3 inherited
    4 inventions 5 detector 6 disappointment
    7 carelessness 8 relief

11 1 spill 2 swallowed 3 taste 4 virus
    5 appliances 6 remote

12 1 on 2 off, into 3 on 4 down 5 in 6 out
    7 out 8 up 9 up 10 down

GRAMMAR

1 1 in order to/to   5 so
   2 so   6 to
   3 to   7 so
   4 in order to/to   8 so

2 1 of, to   5 for   8 of, to
   2 for, for 6 to   9 of, to
   3 of   7 of, to 10 to
   4 for

3 1 If I buy …   5 I often forget …
   2 … enjoyed spicy food. 6 if I spent …
   3 We'll go …   7 When I go …
   4 I'll phone you …   8 we'll have …

4 1 had to   5 don't hurry, will be
   2 have   6 would not eat, was/were
   3 finish   7 will go, don't eat
   4 will catch 8 don't turn down, will boil over

5 1 b 2 a 3 d 4 c 5 b 6 a 7 b 8 d 9 c
   10 b

7 1 are presented   5 has been made
   2 is being upgraded   6 are taught
   3 were both damaged   7 was flooded
   4 has been changed,   8 will be recovered
     was broken into,
     were stolen

8 1 Five new computers were installed in our
     office yesterday.
   2 Our computer network will be checked for
     viruses next week.
   3 The flaw in the computer network wasn't
     detected in time.
   4 The new photocopier was delivered this
     morning.
   5 Schoolchildren are screened for dental
     problems twice a year.
   6 The man was sentenced to five years in prison.
   7 Computers should be installed in all
     classrooms.
   8 The Internet shouldn't be censored.

Lessons 13–15

VOCABULARY

1 customary healthy recognisable faithful
   remarkable memorable wealthy ecstatic
   furious worried/worrying produced ancestral
   farming educated traditional beneficial
   materialistic powerful enthusiastic nervous
   delightful/delighted stressful

2
1 enthusiastic   5 stressful
2 beneficial, productivity 6 healthy
3 power, furious   7 delighted
4 worried   8 ancestors, customs

3 1 d 2 e 3 a 4 c 5 b 6 f

4 1 b 2 c 3 a 4 b 5 d 6 c 7 d 8 b 9 d
      10 b

5 **Feelings:** distraught thrilled upset grateful
      nervous fed-up frustrated inspired peculiar
      Behaviour: far-fetched racist bizarre pathetic
      fascinating eccentric peculiar

6 1 far-fetched 2 uneventful 3 wealthy
      4 elegant 5 boring 6 grateful

7 1 g 2 f 3 h 4 j 5 k 6 b 7 d 8 c
      9 a 10 e 11 i

8 *Example answers:*
1 The early pioneers from Europe established
   themselves on the east coast.
2 They were were dressed in traditional Amish
   costume.
3 Visitors are requested to take their shoes off
   and wash their feet prior to entering the sacred
   building.
4 Cars and motorbikes are banned from the town
   centre.
5 There is no substitute for the hand-written
   letter for personal mail.
6 What is the point in being connected to e-mail?
7 They are easily recognisable as Amish from
   their unusual dress.
8 I fetched my laptop computer from the office.
9 She's on her way to the airport now.
10 If only I hadn't behaved so badly.

GRAMMAR

1
1 are being taught   5 Being connected
2 be shown   6 To be contacted
3 be given   7 being censored
4 being overheard   8 being targeted

2
1 … his phone to be disconnected.
2 … be sent e-mails rather than letters.
3 … to be upgraded.
4 His computer is being checked …
5 … to be mended.
6 …must be informed of the company
   reorganisation plan.
7 … should be introduced to protect consumers.
8 … being faxed a lot of junk mail.

3 1 who 2 whose 3 which 4 who 5 where
      6 which 7 which 8 whose

4 **Defining:** 1 3 4 5 7
      Non-defining: 2 6 8

5
1 The family living next door …
2 The computers controlling the …
3 I worked in a furniture shop situated …
4 We wrote a letter explaining …
5 I have never met the people working for the
   company.

6
1 The place I work at is …
2 The hotel she is staying at is …
3 The flat I live in is …
4 The place he goes to at the weekend …

7 1 f 2 d 3 b 4 a 5 c 6 e

8
1 The person who came to the office …
2 The house where my friends live, is on …
3 She's worried about being charged too much.
4 The media shouldn't be censored.
5 She's the fashion writer whose articles …
6 If she hadn't been delayed, …
7 He could have been hurt badly …
8 If only I had phoned my mother …
9 I wish I had gone with you.
10 I wish I could get a better-paid job.

9 *Example answers:*
1 If it hadn't escaped, it wouldn't have bitten the
   cat.
   I wish I hadn't bought a snake from the pet
   shop.

2 I wouldn't have been burgled if I hadn't let
   the person from the telephone company into
   the house.
   I should have asked the person for some
   identification.

3 If I hadn't been in a two-seater plane, I
   wouldn't be frightened of flying today.
   If only I weren't frightened of flying.

4 I wouldn't have had a fine for bald tyres if the
   police officer hadn't stopped me for speeding.
   I shouldn't have been speeding.

Lessons 16–18

VOCABULARY

1 1 perform 2 bass 3 guitar 4 hit 5 popular
  6 pianist 7 rhythm 8 portrayal

2 1 abroad 2 trip 3 currency 4 notes 5 cash
  6 credit card 7 commission 8 withdrawals
  9 amount 10 exchange 11 transaction
  12 cheque 13 traveller's cheques 14 cash
  15 refundable

3 1 f 2 e 3 a 4 g 5 j 6 d 7 i 8 b
  9 c 10 h

4 1 savings 2 reduction, increased 3 generously
  4 immensely 5 seriousness 6 unnecessary
  7 luxury 8 artificial

5 1 take 2 let/run 3 make 4 put 5 run 6 set
  7 take 8 break 9 get 10 make 11 look
  12 make 13 put 14 take 15 get 16 set
  17 get 18 do 19 take 20 come

6 1 let her down   5 got her own back
  2 taken for granted   6 did her best
  3 made such a fuss of her 7 ran a business
  4 broke his heart   8 get rid of the car

7 1 up   6 up with
  2 up with, for   7 up, away
  3 out of   8 down
  4 into, away with 9 off
  5 up   10 without, away

8 *Example answers:*
  1 bread 2 water 3 toothpaste 4 tomatoes
  5 flowers 6 eggs 7 table-mats 8 clothing
  9 cake 10 shoes 11 cigarettes 12 matches
  13 sardines 14 bread

9 1 b 2 d 3 a 4 c 5 d 6 a 7 b 8 b

10 1 asked for   4 brought up
   2 put off   5 get over
   3 turned down

GRAMMAR

1 1 Why did you tear it up?
  2 I turned it down.
  3 He made it up as he was telling it.
  4 He said he would pay it back.
  5 Would you turn it off, please?
  6 She brought it up at the last meeting.

2 **uncountable:** 1 2 4 5 7 8 10 11 13 14 15 16

3 **similar:** 1 2 5 6
  different: 3 4

4 1 … much time …   6 … a great deal of…
  2 … a little foreign currency … 7 … quite a few…
  3 … some bottles …   8 … a dozen eggs…
  4 There's quite a lot of … 9 … enough money…
  5 … not much money …   10 There are…

5 1 enough 2 a few 3 more 4 hardly 5 some 6 any
  7 little 8 much

6 1 will be going   4 be living
  2 will have finished, need 5 will have changed
  3 will have increased   6 will be moving

7 1 will be using computers.
  2 I will be attending the seminar.
  3 They will have taken off by now.
  4 … many species will have disappeared.

8 1 Personally   5 Amazingly
  2 In my opinion/   6 In my opinion
    To my mind   7 Unfortunately
  3 In my experience   8 In conclusion
  4 In fact

Lessons 18–20

VOCABULARY

1 1 carry on   5 won't let you down
  2 broke into,   6 handing out
    got away with   7 They set out to
  3 broke down   8 we've run out of tea
  4 stands for

2 **Past times:** battle bravery castle chivalry
  king knight legend medieval sword
  The sea: cliffs coast drown float harbour
  mainland sink tide wave wreck
  Christianity: bells ceremony church
  monastery saint spire temple worship

4 1 king 2 tide 3 wreck 4 sword 5 monastery
  6 chivalry 7 saint 8 drown

5 1 spending 2 created 3 reduce, increase
  4 understaffed 5 lower 6 reduce
  7 elections, opposition 8 referendum

6 1 relatively 2 reliable 3 representation
  4 imagination 5 disappeared 6 refreshments
  7 advertising 8 economical 9 sales
  10 simplicity 11 considerate 12 knowledgeable

7 global brand sell product image appeal
  promote message slogan campaign

8 laugh   scream   sing   mutter   shout   groan
stammer   whisper

9 1 laugh   2 whisper   3 scream   4 shout
5 mutter   6 groan

12 1 b   2 d   3 c   4 a   5 d   6 b   7 c   8 d

13 1 car   2 breakfast cereal   3 suitcases
4 toothpaste   5 exercise bicycle   6 mobile phone

14 *Example answers:*
   1 The car is very pleasant to drive.
   2 The cereal will give you a good start to the
     day.
   3 You will look stylish if you travel with one of
     these suitcases.
   4 This toothpaste will make your teeth white and
     shiny.
   5 If you use this exercise bicycle you will get fit
     at home.
   6 This low cost phone will connect you
     anywhere in the world.

GRAMMAR

1 1 They were going to take action to reduce
     urban pollution.
   2 They were going to improve healthcare.
   3 They were not going to increase income tax.
   4 They were going to develop closer links with
     Europe.
   5 They weren't going to reduce public spending
     on defence.

2 1 i   2 d   3 j   4 f   5 a   6 b   7 g   8 e
   9 c   10 h

3 1 She apologised for being out when they called
     that morning.
   2 She advised them to lock all their doors and
     windows.
   3 He suggested inviting some friends over the
     following evening.
   4 She complained to the sales assistant that the
     radio she had bought the previous week was
     already broken.
   5 She warned her children not to walk so near
     the edge of the cliff in case they slipped.
   6 She asked for a receipt.
   7 She offered Peter a lift into town.
   8 She admitted that she had been a bit unfair
     with the children.

4 1 She decided to
     ask …
   2 … the Titanic to sink …
   3 … have been built …
   4 It is believed
     dishonest …
   5 It was so cold …
   6 They insisted on
     taking …
   7 They couldn't decide
     whether to buy …
   8 … to us by a
     dealer …

5 1 It must have been Anna.
   2 It can't have been your father.
   3 They may have lived in Ireland.
   4 He might have studied chemistry.
   5 She must have had a nightmare.

6 1 It is hoped that this Government will do better
     than its predecessor.
   2 It is acknowledged that they are the best
     team …
   3 It is believed that the Loch Ness monster …
   4 It is alleged that Achimedes …
   5 It is considered that children …
   6 It is known that regular exercise …

7 1 1 In my opinion   2 Personally   3 Presumably
     4 Fortunately
   2 1 I suppose   2 In fact   3 Of course
     4 On the contrary
   3 1 In my opinion   2 definitely   3 It is obvious
     4 as a result